SimpleCents Guide to Manage Your Money

How a 7-Day System Can Help You Get Out of Debt, Save 1000's and Build Security – Without Limiting Your Choices, Even if You Can't Budget

D1570574

Written By
SimpleCents

By reading this document, the reader agrees that under no circumstances is the author responsible for any losses, direct or indirect, that are incurred as a result of the use of information contained within this document, including, but not limited to, errors, omissions, or inaccuracies.

FREE BONUS VIDEO COURSE!

The Set It And Forget It Money System

How 4 Easy Steps In Less Than 33 Minutes Will Set Your Money On Autopilot Without Spending Hours On A Budget Even If You Hate Tracking Your Finances

http://www.SimpleCentsMoney.com/VideoCourse

Table of Contents

INTRODUCTION

"Too many people spend money they haven't earned to buy things they don't want to impress people that they don't like." – by Will Rogers

So, What Exactly Is the Big Deal About Managing Money, Anyway? Why Should I Care?

The witty aphorism above by Will Rogers holds more truth than many of us are willing to admit. Let's face it: keeping up with the Joneses, long upheld as an American ideal and a tenuous yet supposedly undeniable marker of the concept that you've "got it made," is a financially (and frankly— psychologically) exhausting task, and attempting to do so has placed a great many Americans in a never ending cycle of debt, stress, and depression with little reward or benefit.

But let's say you aren't trying to keep up with the Joneses. You go through life caring for your needs and the occasional (but not too frequent) want, but you still find yourself inexplicably buried under an ever-increasing mountain of debt. And no matter how much you try to get yourself out of debt, your efforts are utterly futile.

Or perhaps you lost your job, became saddled with a wholly unmanageable medical bill, had an accident, or experienced some other sort of unforeseeable financial disaster which left you with a staggering number of bills to pay and few resources to pay them.

Exactly how you ended up here is beside the point (we'll get into that later). What matters most is how you will get yourself out of this situation. Maybe you are sick of making minimum payments that have no effect whatsoever in terms of lowering the total amount you owe. Or you are fed up with getting rejected for credit applications. Or, you might be tired of feeling like you are barely making it (or not even close to making it) every month or every pay period. Whatever the reason may be, if you have finally come to the realization that something in your life desperately needs to change, then kudos. By reading this guide, you are taking a step in the right direction, your first step toward freeing yourself of debt and building a secure and stable financial future for yourself.

How Reading This Book Will Benefit You

So, what exactly does this guide offer? In short, it contains the recipes for getting yourself out of debt, managing your money properly, and gaining financial wellbeing and stability. All these recipes combine to forge a path to lasting wealth, but not in a risky, speculative manner.

Let's be clear from the start: this is by no means a "get rich quick" book. The step by step solutions in this book are real, but they are not necessarily easy to implement. This will take a great deal of good old-fashioned hard work and determination. But if digging your way out of debt were easy, you wouldn't need to read this book. Don't worry. With some self-awareness, a properly adjusted mindset, and some discipline, the steps detailed in this guide will lead you to the green pastures of financial stability and wealth.

Here's some even better news: although taking the steps in this book to *get yourself out* of debt will be no easy task, *staying* out of debt and maintaining your financial security while building stable wealth for yourself will be easy.

Why is this the case? Well, simply because the change in your mindset and the habits required for you to pay off your debt form the solid foundation for keeping your debt-free status and building greater financial security for yourself. In other words, the hardest part will be setting your mind and forming the habits necessary for getting yourself out of debt. Once your mindset has been transformed, and your habits have become established, many of those same habits will not only rid you of debt but will also allow you to start building wealth in a stable, secure manner. The process revealed in the pages of this book, therefore, does not just help you to pay off your debt. It also provides you with the appropriate procedure to ensure that no matter what life may throw at you, you will not run the risk of falling into debt again, because you will be *prepared* for it.

That's what this book will do for you. It won't just get you out of debt. It will teach you the proper methods of managing your money so that you *stay* out of debt (no matter what happens in life) and begin to build stable and secure wealth for yourself.

What This Book Will Teach You

The first chapter of this book will cover the basics regarding why people get into debt, including the number one reason (which nobody likes to admit).

The second chapter will underscore your basic need: to have a change in your mindset regarding the concept of debt as well as your spending habits. You won't be able achieve a major change in your life without first having a major change in your mindset. Chapter two also goes over exactly what your new mindset should be.

Chapter three through chapter nine can be considered the heart of this book. They provide you with a comprehensive, step by step and day by day approach for getting out of debt. This step by step plan is broken into seven days, one chapter per day. Each day, you will implement the next step of the plan. In just one week, you can lay the foundation for getting out of debt and for your own financial independence and security.

Chapter ten summarizes the seven-day plan and goes over the debt management mistakes you should avoid so you don't jeopardize your path to building wealth and financial stability.

Chapter eleven deals with the danger of credit cards, as well as how to wean yourself off these financial traps.

We said earlier that chapters three through nine constitute the heart of the book, with that comprehensive, seven-day plan for getting out of debt. But chapter twelve contains the secret for *staying* out of debt, and chapter thirteen builds on that by describing practical ways to save money.

Finally, chapter 15 offers you some practical and altogether doable tips on wading into the world of investing, which will help you to achieve your long-term goal of building wealth and financial security. By educating yourself thoroughly on the fundamentals of investing, you will not fall into the trap of trying to get rich quick through high risk investments. Careful planning and sticking to reliable, tried and true investment strategies will be the key to your investment success.

Who Is SimpleCents? And Why Should You Listen to SimpleCents?

The SimpleCents team works tirelessly to provide readers with access to reliable, verified, and regularly updated information on financial management. The niche specialization of the members of our team ensures that SimpleCents is well equipped to provide you, the reader, with the best and most authoritative information. In fact, teaching people about the core fundamentals of money management in a way that is both approachable and easy to master is one of our passions.

Let's be clear: we couldn't be more excited about helping you to take this journey toward financial wellness, security, and independence. This book, like everything else SimpleCents offers, focuses on offering everyday folks like you the practical, actionable information needed in order to dig yourself out of that debt hole, better your financial situation, and improve the quality of your life through an elevation of your financial wellbeing. We know how much it sucks to be in that debt hole, to feel like you're in a downward spiral that you can't claw your way out of, no matter how hard you try. That's why we are so committed to helping you by providing you with practical, doable, achievable steps to financial wellness. We admit that it won't be the easiest thing in the world (especially when it comes to establishing sound financial habits). But if you are willing to heed the steps described in this book and commit yourself to follow through, we promise that it will be altogether worth your while.

It was Teddy Roosevelt who stated, "Nothing in the world is worth having or worth doing unless it means effort, pain, difficulty... I have never in my life envied a human being who led an easy life. I have envied a great many people who led difficult lives and led them well." So, although following the plan in this book to achieve financial security and build wealth may not be easy, what you gain will certainly be altogether valuable and worthy of your efforts.

This is the second book in SimpleCents' personal finance series due to the critical importance of getting one's debt under control when seeking to establish one's financial health and well-being. Being saddled with debt is a huge obstacle in the pursuit of wealth and financial stability, so we want to set you on the right path when it comes to these crucial matters.

The contents of this book detail the procedures and strategies which have been successfully utilized by thousands of people over the years to rid themselves of crippling debt and better their financial standing. SimpleCents is not attempting to peddle some proprietary formula for paying off your debt and building financial stability and wealth. Instead, our team offers you tried and true methods, sound, tested advice, divided up into manageable chunks which can be followed with relative ease, thus turning the seemingly impossible and Herculean task of paying off all the debt that you owe into a fairly manageable and altogether achievable process.

Following the steps outlined in this book is your ticket to a debt-free, financially secure future. So, what are you waiting for? Let's dive in!

Chapter 1

WHAT EVERYBODY OUGHT TO KNOW ABOUT BEING IN DEBT

Turning your financial troubles around starts with some self-awareness. To initiate a life-changing journey, you must understand why you are where you stand right now. The reasons for getting in debt and staying in it are just a few and the first chapter will outline the most common ones, the ones which apply to the vast majority of us.

Most People Are in Debt Due to One Simple Reason – They Spend More Money Than They Make

The reason most people are in debt is incredibly simple, but it is rarely pointed out: They spend more money than they make. Much of the time, your debt problem stems from this one simple cause.

More than 40% of Americans spend more money than they earn due to credit cards and loans

Unfortunately, spending more money than you make is an extremely common practice. In fact, in the United States, over 40 percent of us spend more money than we make, which leads to a financial life centered which is centered on debt. If you also tend to spend more money than you make, you are essentially selling your income to the future. If you do not have a plan in place designed for catching up to the amount of the money that you have spent already, then the debt that you run up will then begin to accumulate even more debt due to the interest which will be charged. You are probably all too familiar with the vicious cycle that results from interest (and the compounding of interest). When you run up debt, eventually, you will most likely end up paying interest on your interest. Unfortunately, this lifestyle of spending more than you make serves only to perpetuate the myth that in the future, you will be able to catch up on your debt, a myth which helps to keep you, year after year, in the same exact situation as you were before.

Even some of the most credit savvy and disciplined consumers are liable to fall into debt in less than the blink of an eye. Even if spending more than what you earn is not the issue for you, you or someone in your household may become affected by a personal emergency. Financial experts typically recommend that you keep a savings fund equal to expenses of at least six months in order to be able to cover for unforeseen emergency costs, but due to the fact that less than 6 percent on average of American incomes go toward savings, most of the costs of the personal emergencies that people face need to be financed, placed on a credit card or covered through a loan of some kind.

The lack of a payment plan and the accumulation of interest creates a vicious cycle

The vicious cycle which is created by the lack of a payment plan and the accumulation of interest is a downward spiral that can be extremely difficult to get yourself out of. Let us examine some of the consequences of interest and how it can quickly cause things to spin out of your control by looking at an example.

Here is how the interest rate on a credit card works:

The interest rate listed on your credit card statement or in the terms and conditions of that credit card is spoken of on a yearly basis, in annual terms. (The term "APR" stands for annual percentage rate.) Your credit card company will use the daily rate (which is defined as the APR on your credit card divided by 365) to apply the interest, it charges to your credit card account balance. The issuer of your credit card then uses that calculated daily figure by multiplying the balance of your account at the end of every day by that figure throughout the duration of the billing cycle.

For instance, if your credit card has an annual rate of 20%, the daily rate for your card would equal 0.05479%. If you have a balance of $1,000, you would be incurring interest of $0.55, resulting in a total of $1,000.55 on the following day. For most credit cards, the interest is compounded. This means that even if you spend no money on the following day, the interest for that day is charged on the $1,000.55, not the $1,000. You end up paying interest on your interest. This process goes on as you continue carrying a balance on your credit card and making new purchases through the month's end. If you had a balance of $1,000 at the start of the month and did not make any other purchases or incur any other charges for the remainder of that month, you would end up having a credit card bill of $1,017.12 by the end of the month. For the sake of illustration, if you incur no other charges on that credit card and make no payments on that card for the rest of the year, you will end up with a total credit card balance of $1221.34 after 365 days. Now, the actual figure after one year would be less than that due to the fact that you would be making at least the minimum payment on the account each month; a credit card company would never let you get away with not making any payments on the account for an entire year. But do you see the dangers of interest and compounded interest? You do not just pay 20% interest on that $1,000 (which would equal $200). You pay more than 20% interest, since the interest is compounded. In the above illustration, you would pay $221.34 in interest after one year.

Given that the average credit card interest rate in the US as of June 2020 is 20.09% and the average credit card balance in the first quarter of 2020 was $8,509, you can see how drastically interest can accumulate. For instance, if we apply the conditions from the example above using these actual figures, after a month, the balance would be $8,655.39 (which equates to $146.39 in interest), and after a year, the balance would be a staggering $10,401.69 (which means that you would be paying $1,892.69 in interest for the year)! And that is without making any additional purchases for the rest of the year. It is easy to see why so many typical American consumers are drowning in debt. The astronomically high interest rates on credit cards make it all too easy for us to fall behind on paying back our debt.

The lesson learned here is this: If you carry a balance on your credit card, it can get very expensive over time due to the interest and the compounded interest. This is why you should always try your best to pay the balance on your credit card in full each month. Due to the staggeringly high interest rates which are charged by credit card companies, it just does not make mathematical sense to carry a credit card balance (especially if you have any savings elsewhere). But, as we will discuss shortly, many Americans do not have savings elsewhere and have no obvious recourse for paying off their credit card balance in full each month.

Many people live from paycheck to paycheck and do not have an emergency fund

Indeed, the debt situation is also often made worse by the fact that many people live from month to month and do not have an emergency fund to cover unexpected expenditures.

Living from month to month or from paycheck to paycheck also generates a situation in which you tend to have nothing on which to fall back if your money happens to run out. As we said before, this lifestyle of spending more than you make serves only to perpetuate the myth that in the future, you will be able to catch up on your debt, a myth which helps to keep you, year after year, in the same exact situation as you were before.

However, in the modern world, spending less than the amount that you earn has not been the behavior model with which many people grow up and are accustomed to, even though paying cash and saving up will keep you in a better position for the future. The income which you earn monthly should not be used for paying for the things that you have already purchased. The money that comes in every month should be reserved for the purchases of that month and that month alone, and a portion of it should be set aside for a savings fund of some kind.

So, what exactly is this savings fund or emergency fund, and what should it look like?

An emergency fund is a quantity of money set aside in a bank account or something similar which can be used to pay for unforeseen (and oftentimes large) expenses, such as major car repairs, the repair or the replacement of major home appliances, unexpected medical expenses, and unemployment or a similar reduction of income (which can be the costliest expense of all).

An emergency fund generates a buffer for you financially which may help to keep you above water in your time of need without causing you to have to take out loans or to rely on credit cards. Such an emergency fund will allow you to stop borrowing more and getting yourself into more debt. However, the practice of having an emergency fund is often ignored or avoided. Look at the following stunning fact:

Only 18% of Americans are confident that they could live off only their savings in the coming six months

Only 18% of Americans are confident that they would be able to live off only their savings in the next six months. In fact, 28% of people report they do not have savings to last them for even one month.

This does not bode well for the debt situation. It means that even if you do not already carry a credit card balance or have other debt in the form of loans, you might still fall quite easily into debt the moment one of those aforementioned emergencies happens to you, because since you lack an emergency fund to cover that unexpected cost, you will be forced to put that expense on a credit card or take out a loan in order to cover it.

Some more troubling statistics

Many Americans would not be able to pay their monthly expenses if they missed just one paycheck. And only 40% of Americans report that they could pay for an unexpected expense of $1,000, such as a car repair or a trip to the emergency room, using only their savings. Most people asked say that they would either take out a personal loan or put that expense on a credit card.

What's even more troublesome is the fact that most emergencies in the United States cost more than $1,000 to address. The average unforeseen expense was reported to be $3,500. Such situations are more common than we may realize. Last year, 28 percent of people had a financial emergency of some kind, and the tumultuous events of the first half of 2020 have served only to increase that number drastically. The US unemployment rate in April of 2020 rose to a record 14.7 percent, meaning that a record-breaking number of people that month experienced one of the costliest emergencies there is: losing a job.

Whether it is due to unemployment or some other reason, the fact of the matter is that due to the lack of a proper emergency fund, many Americans are just one personal emergency away from falling into debt. And many other Americans are already in debt because they spend more than they make.

Some Other Common Reasons Why People Get into Debt

Some other common reasons for getting in debt include the following:

Poor money management

One major reason for getting into debt is poor money management. Here are some examples of poor money management practices, many of which I cover in detail elsewhere in this book:

- Failing to save money
- Failing to pay your bills on time
- Failing to have a budget and to stick to it
- Succumbing to impulse purchases
- Buying the things that you want instead of the things that you need
- Borrowing money and getting into debt
- Keeping up with the Joneses
- Being penny wise and pound foolish
- Failing to learn about sound money management practices

Underemployment or a sudden loss of income

This one may not seem very fair, but, as I discussed earlier, underemployment, a sudden loss of income, or unemployment are other contributing factors why people get into debt. Losing your job, your main source of income, can put any of us in a situation of dire financial distress. But if you live from paycheck to paycheck and don't have anything that even remotely resembles an emergency fund, you are even more liable to fall into debt when you experience a sudden loss of income, as you may be forced to turn to credit cards or high interest loans in order to cover your essential expenses.

A lack of understanding as to how credit cards and loans work

Also, a lack of understanding as to how credit cards and loans work can contribute to your being in debt. For instance, selecting the wrong financial instruments which may come with highly unfavorable conditions or far too high of an interest rate) will certainly contribute to the accumulation of debt. We will cover this in detail later, but before you decide to take on a loan or a new credit card, you must carefully peruse the terms and conditions and develop a clear and thorough understanding of them. Do not jump into anything without careful planning and understanding. In other words, look before you leap.

Only paying the minimum on loans debt, which prolongs the vicious cycle

If you pay only the minimum amount due on your loan debt and your credit card debt, this gets you further into debt and prolongs the vicious cycle of debt due to the accumulation and compounding of interest, as was shown in the example earlier. You may even end up paying only the interest on your debt (and not paying down any of the principle) if you pay only the minimum amount due. For instance, credit card and loan companies usually set their monthly required minimum payments as low as possible. $25 or $35, in our experience, are exceedingly common (and arbitrary) amounts for minimum payments on credit cards. But remember the example we gave earlier? Here's a refresher: The average credit card interest rate in the US as of June 2020 is 20.09%, and the average credit card balance in the first quarter of 2020 was $8,509. If we apply the conditions from the example above using these actual figures, after a month, the balance would be $8,655.39 (which equates to $146.39 in interest). If that credit card has a monthly minimum payment of $35 and you pay only that minimum payment, then you are left with a balance of $8620.39. The $35 that you paid would not even come close to covering the interest accrued on your balance that month, let alone paying down your principle. In reality, if you are carrying a balance of $8,509 on a single credit card, your monthly minimum payment will likely be set at a higher number, such as $150. But even if we account for this higher minimum payment, you still have a balance of $8,505.39 after making that $150 minimum payment. Because the interest charged that month was $146.39, this means that almost all of that $150 went toward paying the interest on your balance, and only $3.61 of your payment went toward the principle of your debt.

So, paying merely the minimum payment due each month on your credit cards and loans is an excellent way to keep yourself in debt for quite a long time. The 2009 Credit Card Accountability Responsibility and Disclosure (CARD) Act requires that credit card companies issue a "Minimum Payment Warning" to cardholders on every statement. It tells you how long it will take to pay off the balance on your credit card if you make no additional charges on the card and you pay only the minimum payment. It also informs you how much extra you will pay in terms of credit card interest if you pay only the minimum payment. Lastly, it tells you how much you need to pay each month (assuming that no additional charges are made on the card) in order to pay off the balance in three years and also informs you of how much you will save in terms of interest if you do this.

Having adopted the mindset that being in debt is a normal part of life

Accepting as fact the thought that it is normal to be in debt is yet another reason you may have gotten yourself into debt. You must reject such a mindset. It is not normal or healthy to be in debt. Despite the fact that you and everyone else around you seems to be in debt or to treat debt as a normal part of life, believing that credit card and loan debt is normal is a poor money management practice and an improper mindset which keeps you stuck in that vicious cycle of debt by decreasing your level of motivation for getting yourself out of debt.

Having your expenses increase as soon as your income goes up

This one is simple. Let us say that your spending each month already outstrips your income, as is the case for many Americans. If you start spending more money as soon as your income increases, you will continue to remain in debt. That promotion, pay raise, or side gig will do you no good in terms of getting yourself out of debt if you spend the increase as soon as you have it.

Additional Resources

- https://www.lifehack.org/articles/money/15-reasons-why-youre-debt.html
- https://www.lifehack.org/articles/money/7-causes-people-get-into-debt.html
- https://www.debt.com/news/how-do-people-get-into-debt/

- https://money.howstuffworks.com/personal-finance/debt-management/reason-people-go-into-debt.htm
- https://money.usnews.com/money/personal-finance/debt/articles/9-reasons-youre-still-in-debt
- https://www.moneycrashers.com/reasons-get-out-debt/

Chapter 2

GET RID OF YOUR DEBT ONCE AND FOR ALL

Now that you have a better understanding of your situation and exactly how you ended up here, it is time to pinpoint the best approaches for getting out of debt. The first thing you need to realize is that there are no quick fix solutions to the problem of debt. Rather, a change in your mindset and some brand-new habits will be required.

What You Actually Need in Order to Start Getting Rid of Your Debt: A Change in Your Mindset

Most people know they need to spend less and save more. Thus, just telling someone to do so is not going to work. A shift in mindset is required to start embracing financial responsibility. And once this happens, getting out of debt starts requiring a lot less effort.

Below are seven vital shifts in your mindset that you must undergo as you are paying down your debt.

Forgive yourself for making the decision that led you into debt

There is really no point in beating yourself up about it. Perhaps you are in debt through no fault of your own (for instance, your spouse had a medical emergency that wasn't covered by health insurance) or perhaps you are in debt because you got into the habit of going on far too many shopping sprees. Or you bought that TV because you really wanted it (and felt like you needed it) and you were lured by the attractive financing options.

It doesn't matter what happened to you or what poor (or even normal) decisions you may have made to land yourself in debt. There really is not a point in beating yourself up for decisions that you made in the past. You should leave no room whatsoever for these kinds of thoughts. To a certain extent, it doesn't matter how you got here. (I say "to a certain extent" because you do need to stop the behavior that landed you in debt in the first place, such as spending more than you make.) But what matters most is what you are going to do about it now. Do not waste any more time harping on past errors of judgment. We have all been there at one point or another; we are human, after all. Don't waste your energy feeling bad about it. Use that mental energy to make a solemn determination that you are going to get yourself out of debt.

Every bit counts when you are paying off your debt

Don't be discouraged by what you may perceive as slow progress, which sometimes seems like no progress at all. If you stick to the procedure detailed in this book, you will see results — not immediately, but you will see them. Paying off just one card is actual progress. Even just a few dollars a month toward your emergency fund is progress. Pay off as much as you can, but don't feel dejected if you do not see an immediate effect or an instantaneous rise in your credit score.

You are not the sum of your debts

You should not consider your debt to reflect who you are as a human being. Do not be defined by the stigma or the shame of being in debt. It is not who you are. It is a condition that you are in, true, but you are actively working to get yourself out of it.

Assume the responsibility for the debt that you owe

Do not blame other people, things, or events for your debt. No one else has to deal with it, so it is not a productive use of your time or energy to place the blame on others. Even if it is truly not your fault, you are the one who has to live with it, so just take responsibility for it. And don't blame the person who got you into debt (if that is the case). That will only poison your relationship with them and cause resentment, which will do nothing towards paying off your debt.

Express some gratitude for the debts that you owe

This one may seem a bit far-fetched. Debt is by no means a positive thing (or else we wouldn't have written this whole book on how to get yourself out of debt and stay out of debt). But as you are paying off your debt, take a moment to consider what you gained from getting yourself into debt. Perhaps you have student loans. Consider the experience you gained from that degree and the value of your education. Maybe you bought a car. Think about all the good times you have had in that car, all the places you have been in it. If you spent too much money on clothes, take a moment to consider all the amazing times you had in those stunning outfits. If you went on a trip that was a tad too extravagant, scroll through some of the pictures of that trip and revel in the fond memories.

If you look at your debt from this angle, you may have an easier time as you are paying it off, and the memories may bring you more happiness.

Do whatever it takes—nothing is beneath you when you are paying off your debt.

If you can get a part time job that fits into your schedule and will provide you with extra money for paying down your debt, do it (even if it involves cleaning bathrooms). Don't consider such a thing beneath your dignity. Remember: this is a temporary situation that you are putting yourself in so that you can reap the rewards (being free of debt) later. Skip those weekend jaunts with your friends. With the extra time, you can get a side gig instead. Just do whatever it takes to meet your debt paying goals. The reward will be worth your while.

Do not try to go it alone

You are not alone. The statistics mentioned in the previous chapter make that abundantly clear. So, there is no need to act like you are the only person going through this.

Get an accountability partner, someone to keep you accountable as you are paying off your debts. This will be discussed in detail in chapter nine.

Also, if you need to rant to someone about your debt, find a friend who will listen to you (and who may be in the same situation). Sometimes, you might just need to vent, rant, or talk it through. You don't have to be a lone ranger, suffering through this by yourself. Many other people are going through the same thing, and you can reach out to them for mental and emotional support.

As you are paying down your debt, the proper mindset is critical. Undergoing the above shifts in your mindset will help to make the entire process easier and much more bearable. If you apply these changes to your way of thinking and follow the rest of the procedure discussed in this book, you will be okay (more than okay). So, don't worry too much. Just apply yourself in the manner described. You have to do it; no one will do it for you. Realize this.

Start Changing Your Priorities and Goals

To pay down your debt, you will need to start changing your priorities and goals in life.

Learn to combat the allure of instant gratification and resist those impulse buys

Impulsive purchases right now provide you with immediate gratification. And unfortunately, our society today is all about instant gratification, with notifications pushed to your smartphone the second that they occur. This instant gratification culture has led to shorter attention spans and an "I want it now" attitude. But that must change. Saving to make a major purchase or to pursue a goal in the future means that you will have to delay your pleasure.

Apply the 24-hour rule

One outstanding way to wean yourself off those impulse buys is to use something called the 24-hour rule. When you are faced with a large purchase, give yourself a cooling off period that lasts 24 hours. Go home, sleep on it, and decide the next day if that purchase is absolutely necessary (after the adrenaline has leveled off).

Taking this 24-hour period to decide if you are going to buy something has the added benefit of allowing you to properly determine if the item is a want or a need.

Learn to evaluate and to separate your wants and your needs

Start evaluating your wants and your needs. How often do you buy something that you want but that you don't really need?

This may be a tough one to deal with, but it is a necessary part of the change in your mindset that you will have to undergo. Take a good, hard, realistic look at your expenses, and separate what you need from what you want.

You may feel like you "need" that Netflix subscription, but let's be honest: you can live without it. As you are paying down your debts, you must be willing to let go of the things that you do not actually need to survive. So, what are your needs? Well, you need food, water, shelter, and clothing.

This means that you need to buy food (but you do not need to eat out at a restaurant—you will save a lot of money by cooking your own food and you will not die if you don't eat at restaurants).

It means that you need to pay your utilities bills: your electricity, gas, water, trash, internet, and phone bills. The last two, your internet bill and your phone bill, might not be an absolute necessity for survival, but the lack of internet or a cell phone will make your life exceedingly difficult in this day and age, especially if people need to contact you for work. So, you can consider your cell phone bill a necessity. But it is not a necessity to have the best plan or the latest smartphone. Go with the cheapest plan that will suit your needs and which will not hinder you from functioning in society. Most people take an internet connection for granted, but if you are truly desirous of saving money and cutting costs, you can choose a much cheaper (and slower) level of service. Or, if you are lucky enough to live near a place with free, dependable Wi-Fi and are willing to forgo a constant Wi-Fi connection at home, then the savings from stopping your internet service can be enormous. Remember: this is only a temporary situation that you are enduring to get yourself out of debt as soon as possible.

It means that you need to pay your rent or your mortgage. But if your rent is one of the major factors contributing to your debt, you may want to consider moving to a place that is more affordable for you. The general recommendation is that you should be spending no more than 30% of your gross income each month on your rent or mortgage payment.

It means that you may need to go shopping for clothes occasionally. But let's be clear: you probably already have plenty of clothes to wear for your normal daily situations, and you most likely do not need to buy more clothes for a while. Perhaps if all your socks or underwear have holes; you might need to purchase some of those necessities. But this is a category that most adults do not really *need* to spend money on, as they already have more than enough to cover themselves. When you are paying down your debt, buy what you need in terms of clothing and do not exceed that boundary. If your rationale for buying something is that you need it because it is "cute," that should raise a huge red flag for you. Put it down and walk away.

Unless you work from home or live within walking distance of all the places you need to go, you also need some form of transportation. If you have a car, you need to pay those car payments and pay for gas and maintenance. If you don't have a car, you might need to buy a ticket for public transportation (if that is an option in the area in which you live). If you do not have a car or a public transit pass but are lucky enough to find a coworker or someone with whom you can carpool, you will need to make regular contributions to that person for his or her gas and maintenance. It's only fair (and polite).

Another need is health insurance. You may already have this through your employer. You may not consider it a need, but you should do so, since you are paying down your debt. A medical emergency not covered by health insurance will quickly erase any and all progress that you have made toward paying down your debt. So, get health insurance.

And of course, an all-important need (especially for those who are paying down debt) is to pay all your bills on time. We will discuss this in detail later.

Everything beyond what was listed above is almost certainly a want, not a need, although it may depend on your circumstances. If, for instance, you work from home, supplies for your home office might be considered needs. You know your own situation. But be brutally honest with yourself when it comes to separating your wants from your needs. We know this can be difficult, but you need to do it regardless.

And after you separate all your wants from your needs, cut out the wants from your expenses. Get rid of basically all your wants. Perhaps occasionally (once every two or three months), you can eat at your favorite restaurant. But you should stop spending money on anything that is a want rather than a need. You can give yourself a bit of encouragement in the form of a "want" reward for meeting some of your debt paying milestones. For instance, you can perhaps allow yourself to eat at said restaurant or buy that item you have been wanting to buy once you meet a particular debt goal or pay off that account by the date you fixed for yourself. Just make sure that the reward, the want, is not expensive and will not set back the progress you have made in paying down your debt.

Figure out how much you spend every month (realistically!)

Do a realistic assessment of how much you spend during a month. How does that number compare to the income you earn? Unless you track their spending over a certain time period, you may not have any idea about how much money you are actually wasting on those impulse buys or those wants (an average person may spend $450 per month or $5,400 per year on impulse purchases). Do your best to cut down your spending so that your spending each month does not outstrip your income.

Keep the bigger picture in mind

Doing such an assessment for a couple of months while also focusing on bigger goals for the future, (buying a house, starting your own business, traveling the world) can help you to start changing your way of thinking. When you get into a more financially savvy mindset, you are taking a crucial step in terms of working toward getting out of debt.

A Comprehensive, Step by Step Approach for Getting Out of Debt

The next several chapters cover a comprehensive, step by step approach for getting out of debt. When executed correctly, this system can introduce workable change towards a debt-free existence in just seven days. Read on to discover the recipe for enacting genuine and long-lasting financial change in your life.

Chapter 3

A COMPREHENSIVE, STEP BY STEP APPROACH FOR GETTING OUT OF DEBT: DAY 1 – CHECK YOUR CREDIT SCORE AND CREDIT REPORT IN ORDER TO GET A BETTER SENSE OF WHERE YOU CURRENTLY STAND FINANCIALLY

Much of the information in this chapter is excerpted from the *SimpleCents Guide to Credit Repair*. If you would like to know more about the concept of credit and about how you can improve your credit score (which is an excellent way to improve your financial wellbeing and set you on the path toward building wealth), we strongly recommend the aforementioned guide.

What Is A Credit Report? What Is A Credit Score? Why Are These Important?

First, what is credit? Credit is what gives you the ability to buy goods or services with the agreement that you will pay for it later or over time. Unless you are among those who can pay for everything in cash from your food and groceries to your car and house, you'll more than likely need to use credit at one point or another in your life. Credit is the actual ability that you must borrow money to buy goods or services, not be confused with your credit score or credit report.

Your credit score is a snapshot of your financial situation that helps lenders and creditors decide how trustworthy you are to pay them back. Your credit score is the number describing your use of credit throughout the years — it represents a record of how you have borrowed money and repaid that money in your past. Credit scores can range from ~300 to 850 (depending on the score model used), and the higher your score is, the more trustworthy you appear to lenders and creditors. While there is a lot of weight put on your credit score, it is just one part of the much bigger picture — the credit report.

The score helps to summarize the entirety of the credit report to give potential lenders a quick glimpse at your credit history. The actual credit report details each line of credit that you have. Not only do credit reports provide lenders and creditors with details about your lines of credit, but they will also let them know of any major financial issues you've recently had such as bankruptcies, foreclosures, and repossessions. A credit report is something you should start checking regularly to make sure there isn't any inaccurate information that could be affecting you how you appear to lenders.

What about FICO? FICO Scores were created more than thirty years ago with the Fair Isaac Corporation — the namesake for the FICO Score. The purpose behind creating FICO Scores was to create a standardized credit score that would it make easier for lenders and creditors to get an idea of someone's creditworthiness. So, a FICO Score is a credit score that is known and used to judge whether your credit is good or bad.

Before FICO Scores became the industry standard, there were all sorts of credit scores with all sorts of ways to calculate them. This made it difficult for people to receive loans and borrow money with the best interest rates since you didn't know what was going into your credit score. In the early days of credit scores, your gender and political affiliation would be used to help calculate your score, neither of which has anything to do with your creditworthiness.

FICO Scores are three-digit numbers that are calculated based on probabilities and statistical analysis using the information found in your credit reports. This is why it's so important that you monitor your credit reports compiled by the three credit bureaus because that's how your credit score is calculated.

The easiest way to think about a FICO Score is as a quick summary of your credit report. When you apply for a loan or credit card, the lenders can take a glance at your FICO Score to help them quickly determine if they want to loan you money and also what interest rate they will charge on that money. FICO Scores help quicken this process because lenders can see a summary for your credit reports in one three-digit number and know if they want to take a deeper look into your credit history or if they don't have interest in loaning you money at all.

Don't think that FICO Scores are only beneficial to the lenders and creditors, however, they also make the entire process fairer for you as well. As mentioned previously, before FICO Scores became the industry standard, your credit score was calculated in so many different ways that it was impossible to keep track of and know exactly what you needed to do to bring that score up — as it could change from bank to bank without you doing anything differently.

With FICO Scores, you can learn about exactly how they're calculated so that you can do what's needed to boost that score up. There are well-known guidelines for how the score is calculated and proven methods for raising it.

Let's look at how FICO Scores are calculated. Now that you know what FICO Scores are and everything you ever wanted to know about the different versions of FICO Scores — probably more than you want to know about the different versions — let's dive into what's really important here: how FICO Scores are calculated. By understanding how the scores are determined, you'll learn what you need to do to boost that credit score back up.

According to a study from early 2019, LendingTree found that 2 out of every 5 (37%) Americans don't know how their credit scores are calculated. Not only did they not know how they were calculated, but almost 40% of the country also has no clue how credit scores truly work. Considering how important credit scores and credit, in general, is for everyday life, it's important to know what goes into the calculation.

Don't feel bad if you don't have any idea how credit scores work or how they're calculated, nobody ever teaches us that in regular life. Even those that do have a better understanding of credit in general and know a few things about their scores more than likely don't know everything that goes into it. The good news is that it's simple to learn and understand so that you can improve your credit score the right way.

While everything in your credit reports contributes to your FICO Scores, that information is placed into five groups with different weightings to affect your score. The five main groups are payment history, credit use, length of credit history, new credit/number of accounts, and how your credit is mixed among types. Let's take a deeper dive into each category.

Payment history — 35% of your FICO Score

This is the most widely known factor in determining credit score and the one with the biggest impact on your score. Payment history is the record of how you've made payments on your various lines of credit throughout your time using them, including credit cards, auto loans, mortgages, personal loans, retail credit accounts, and more. Being late on a couple of payments here or there may not crush your score permanently, but it can have a big effect early on. A single delinquent (missed) payment can drop your score by over 100 points! Therefore, it is so important to make sure you keep track of any and all accounts that you have open so you can make payments on time every month.

Missed or late payments are payments that are at least 30 days overdue. Creditors may not report your account as delinquent before this 30-day mark, so if you forget a payment, be sure to pay the offending amount as soon as you remember! (Or just don't forget to pay—refer to Chapter 8 for more details).

Credit use or amounts owed — 30% of your FICO Score

The category with the second biggest impact on your FICO Score is one that people know a lot less about than payment history — credit use. This is a fancy way of saying how much of your total available credit you have used and currently owe back to the lenders and creditors. Accounting for 30% of your FICO Score, this is a hugely important part of your financial life that you should take seriously and understand.

Fundamentally, credit utilization is the percentage of all the credit available to you that you are actually using, or your credit balance divided by your total available credit. Your credit utilization ratio can be calculated in the following manner: take the balance you owe and divide it by your credit limit. Multiply your result by 100 to get the percentage.

For example, if you owe a balance of $200 on a credit card with a credit limit of $1,000, then your utilization for that card is 20%. But if you have a limit of only $500 on that card, then your utilization ratio jumps to 40% with the same balance, since your credit limit is lower, and you are thus using a higher percentage of your available credit.

This can be calculated for one credit card to get your utilization ratio for just that card, or it can be done for all the debt you owe to get your overall credit utilization ratio. Credit scoring models will take into account your overall credit utilization ratio (the sum of all the debt you owe divided by the total amount of credit available under your name multiplied by 100) and may also consider the individual credit utilization ratios for each of your credit cards and loans. To have a good credit score, you should keep your overall credit utilization and the credit utilization for each of your cards under 30%.

Length of credit history — 15% of your FICO Score

Starting the categories with less weight on your FICO Score is the length of credit history. This one is simple to understand, it's exactly what it sounds like. This portion of your FICO Score looks at how long you've had a credit account of any kind. The longer your established credit history, the better your FICO Score will typically be.

Length of credit history is a result of the oldest account you have, the newest, and the average age of all your credit accounts. It can be a bit confusing when trying to lower your credit. Once you pay off one of your oldest accounts, it is better to leave the account open to keep the length of your credit history as long as possible. Closing the account will not only negatively affect your credit history length but also lower the overall amount of credit you have, negatively affecting your credit utilization ratio as well. So, it's usually best to keep an account open (even after you pay it off). Just take measures (like cutting up your credit card) to prevent yourself from running up debt on that account again.

New credit— 10% of your FICO Score

New credit is exactly what it sounds like—opening new lines of credit. Whether it be credit card applications, financing a new car, or buying a house, opening new lines of credit can lower your credit score. This is because every time you apply for any of the above, lenders do a hard inquiry on your credit report so they can see your credit history.

Too many hard inquiries in a short amount of time will lower your credit score as it presents you as a higher risk to lenders. It may seem to them that you are trying to open as many lines of credit as you can to pay for things since you don't have the money or steady income to pay for them outright. This may or may not be true, but that's how it seems when someone tries to open a lot of new credit accounts in a short amount of time.

Credit mix and number of accounts — 10% of your FICO Score

The last main category of your FICO Score is the mix of credit accounts as well as the total number of accounts that you have. It's best to have various account types as well as a decent number of total accounts. This, in conjunction with doing well in the other categories, shows lenders that you can handle a variety of account types and significantly raises your creditworthiness.

Ideally, you will have a mixture of revolving credit and installment credit, with credit cards, a mortgage, auto loans all being present to show that you can make payments on various account types. Also, if you have a fair amount of credit accounts, suggested to have 11-20+, it shows that you are creditworthy and will be able to pay off another account if you choose to open one. It's only good to have this many accounts if all are in good standing — you don't want to have eleven credit accounts that all owe significant balances.

FICO Score Classification

Now that you know everything about how your FICO Score is calculated, let's look at some of the important aspects of your FICO Score. You probably want to know what the scores truly mean to a lender, as well as how you stack up against other people across the industry. FICO Scores are usually referred to as either poor, fair, good, very good, or excellent. This is broken down as follows:

Poor (<580)

If your credit score is under 580, you will be seen by creditors and lenders as having a poor credit score. This score is well below average and tells lenders that you're a very risky borrower. At this range of scores, it is difficult to find a lender willing to loan you money without exorbitant interest rates. According to Experian, 16% of Americans have a credit score that is considered poor.

Fair (580-669)

In this range, lenders will see you as having a fair credit score, even though you are still below the average. With scores in this range, you'll have a much easier time finding lenders willing to loan you money, but you should still expect to pay very high rates on those loans. It is estimated that 17% of Americans have a fair credit score.⟦SEP⟧

Good (670-739)

This range of credit scores will have you crossing the national average of around 706 or being very close to it in either direction. With a good credit score, lenders will be willing to loan your money or open a new credit account with you as you aren't seen as particularly likely to become delinquent any time soon. About 21% of Americans fall into this category.⟦SEP⟧

Very good (740-799)

Once you start getting your credit score above 740, you're entering the category of very good. In this range, you are well above average and lenders will be happy to provide you credit at good interest rates. They'll be confident that you are dependable as a borrower and you'll consistently make payments. The largest portion of Americans falls into this group, about 25%.⟦SEP⟧

Excellent (800+)

If you get your credit score up to over 800, you are doing exceptionally well. Creditors and lenders will be happy to offer you credit with the best interest rates available. You'll be seen as an exceptionally dependable borrower who is almost no risk for money lending. Nearly 21% of all Americans fall into this range.

Number of Credit Bureaus Used

FICO Scores can be calculated based on reports from each of the three main credit bureaus, which is why you can have three different FICO Scores — one from each bureau.

Score Range

As you've seen many times in this book already, FICO Scores range from 300-850 for the general scores, and then industry-specific FICO Scores will range from 250-900. With the FICO Score, a credit score of 670-700+ will qualify you as having good credit.

The good thing about these numbers is that about 2 out of every 3 people in the United States (67%) have a credit score that is good or higher. Don't let that discourage you if you have a credit score that is fair or poor, as this data shows that it is certainly possible to improve your credit score and make it into the higher score brackets. If it wasn't, then there would be far more people in the lower-tiered brackets!

With all the importance placed on credit in the world today, you probably have one main question in mind — why do you need credit? While credit certainly isn't needed for purchasing everything in your life, you will more than likely need it at one point or another. Most people can't afford to go to a car dealership and pay cash for a new car or purchase a couple hundred-thousand-dollar home with cash they pulled out of the bank. Getting loans for these major purchases are a form of credit in themselves, and typically require you to have a credit history, to begin with.

Lenders use your credit history to decide how much they're willing to lend you and what interest rate you'll need to pay them for lending you that money, to begin with. If you don't have any credit, you can expect to get denied loans from many financial institutions outright, and those that do lend you money will likely offer it to you at a high-interest rate. Even if you've always just paid cash for everything and aren't experiencing any discernible financial hardships, it's incredibly important to start establishing a credit history as soon as possible to set yourself up for the best possible interest rates on some of the biggest purchases of your life.

Why Should You Check Your Credit Score and Credit Report?

Your credit scores as well as your credit history are crucial bits of information which are important for your financial health, overall. Seeing your credit scores and credit history as displayed on each of your credit reports will undoubtedly help you to better your present credit position, and thus, your present level of overall financial wellbeing.

Your credit scores as well as your credit history are major factors which potential creditors and lenders—such as mortgage lenders, credit card companies, and auto lenders— use to make their lending decisions. Such companies wish to know the likelihood that you will pay back the money you owe them as was agreed.

Thus, it is important to check both your credit reports and your credit score regularly. These are among the factors which will determine the terms of your loan, including the interest rate, so it is necessary to make sure that the information contained in your credit reports is complete and accurate.

If you are getting ready to buy a new car or home or just trying to stay up to date on your financial status, taking some time to go over your credit scores and your credit reports will help to ready you to take your next step.

How Often Are You Entitled by Law to Check Your Credit Score and Credit Report (For Free)?

By law, you may access your credit report from each of the three credit reporting agencies once per year for free. Below are the details on getting your official credit report and seeing your official credit scores as determined by the major credit bureaus.

According to the Consumer Financial Protection Bureau (CFPB), you are entitled to one free credit report every 12 months from each of the three credit bureaus. This means that in any given year, you can request three credit reports free of charge, one from each bureau.

While you could request all three at the same time and compare them side by side to see the differences between the different agencies, a better option may be to request one every four months. This will enable you to see your credit score throughout the year without having to wait another 12 months to see another official report from any of the three major credit bureaus.

In addition to this one free report per agency every 12 months, you're also entitled to a free credit report if any of the following conditions apply to your life:

- You were denied credit, employment, or insurance based on your credit report and have received written notice. The reporting credit reporting agency must provide you with a free credit report if you request one within 60 days of receiving the notice.
- You are requesting your credit report with the intention of placing an initial fraud alert. You are also able to request a free credit report if you believe that there may be an issue with the report due to fraudulent activity.
- You are currently unemployed but plan to apply for employment within 60 days or submitting your request to obtain your credit report.
- You receive welfare assistance
- Your state has laws that provide for a free credit report.

As you can see, there are many ways that you may be eligible for a free credit report from the three main credit reporting agencies. Even if none of the special conditions apply to you, you're still able to get three free reports per year which should be more than enough to keep an eye on your credit.

How Do You Go About Checking Your Credit Score and Your Credit Report?

Check your credit score/report to get a better idea of your current situation (here's a detailed explanation of how a person can check their credit score: https://www.cnbc.com/select/what-is-a-credit-score-and-how-to-check-yours-for-free/). Also, it's especially important to make sure that your credit report is free from errors. This helps form a baseline of data to see how much debt you have and the whole picture before planning.

Free credit score resources

Most credit card issuers provide free credit score access to their cardholders making it easier than ever to check and know your score.

Some issuers, such as Citi and Discover, provide free FICO Scores, while others, such as Chase and Capital One, provide free VantageScores, which are based on a slightly different credit scoring model (but one with many of the same principles as that of FICO).

You can check your credit score in less than five minutes by logging into your credit card issuer's site or a free credit score service and navigating to the credit score section. There will typically be a dashboard listing your score and the factors that influence it.

FICO and VantageScore will pull your credit score from one of the three major credit bureaus, Experian, Equifax or TransUnion.

Here are some free credit score resources that you can access, whether you're a cardholder or not:

CreditWise from Capital One: Free VantageScore from TransUnion

Chase Credit Journey: Free VantageScore from TransUnion

Discover Credit Scorecard: Free FICO Score from Experian
These resources also provide insight into the key factors affecting your credit score, simulators on how certain actions may affect your credit and helpful tips for improving your credit score.

Okay, So You Checked Your Credit Score and Credit Report. Now What?

Besides figuring out where you stand financially and being able to determine how likely it is that you will be offered and approved for better terms on credit card offers and loans, checking your credit score and credit report is crucial for one other reason: You need to see if there are any errors. Any incorrect information could be negatively affecting your credit score and your overall credit history. Errors may range from simple typos and misspellings to extra accounts that you don't recognize. The latter is a warning sign that you may be a victim of identity theft.

So, peruse your credit report thoroughly for any errors. If there are some, don't worry. The remainder of this chapter will teach you how to correct those errors.

Deleting Items from Your Credit Report

Deleting items from your credit report means having erroneous or false information removed from your credit report that is lowering your score and putting you in a worse financial situation. Well, you should remove any false information from your credit report even if it somehow benefits your credit. You want your credit score to be 100% accurate with how it reflects your life and your finances.

If you've sat down and gone over your credit report in detail – as everyone should on occasion – and you've noticed an issue on your report, it's time to get that taken care of. There is more than one strategy that can be used to take care of this, so let's look at some of the ways to start repairing your credit report.

Find Any Mistakes on Your Credit Reports

Even if you know exactly what information you're looking for when you start examining the credit report because you've seen the inaccurate information, you'll want to examine the entire report with a fine-toothed comb. If you're going through the trouble of disputing one mistake, you should take advantage of it and make sure there are no other mistakes in there that you weren't aware of.

Each time you find a mistake, circle, or highlight it so that you can easily come back to it later when you are disputing the mistake. Make physical copies of the front page of your credit report with all your personal information and copies of the pages with the mistake(s) on them. That way you'll be able to send copies into the credit bureaus and keep copies for yourself. Once you're confident that you've found all mistakes on the credit report, it's time to make the dispute.

File the Dispute

The best way to dispute your credit report is to mail a physical letter to the credit bureau. You want to send these disputes through certified mail and request a return receipt so that you know the credit reporting agency has seen your dispute. In the dispute, you want to type up a letter stating what the issue is, why the information they're reporting is incorrect, and include a copy of the highlighted mistakes that you made earlier so they know exactly what you're referring to.

Wait to Hear Back and Remain Persistent

Once the credit bureaus receive your dispute, they legally have 30 days to address the issue. This could include them right out fixing the issue and everything is peachy, which is the ideal scenario. But you could also wait all this time only to hear back from them stating that the information they're reporting is correct and that they don't intend on fixing the error.

If the bureaus are refusing to fix the mistake — and you're 100% sure that the information is incorrect and you're right — then send another letter stating again why it is incorrect. Also, inform the agencies that you are reporting the same information to the Better Business Bureau, the Consumer Financial Protection Bureau, and your state attorney general (and do so of course!). This is more likely to get the attention of the credit bureau(s) and have them take it more seriously.

Whatever you do, just remain persistent and be patient. It can take a long time to resolve the dispute, but it is more than worth it in the end!

Wait for the Negatives to Expire

The good thing about the negatives on your credit report is that no matter what you do in terms of trying to get them removed, they will eventually stop getting reported on your credit report. This is because the law prohibits negative information on your credit report from being reported for more than 7 years for the vast majority of things. The exception to the 7-year rule are bankruptcies, which can be reported for up to 10 years.

As a bonus, even as you're waiting for the negatives to get off your credit report, they have less and less of an impact on your credit over time. This is because as the old negative information gets replaced with fresh new information that is much better, the new stuff starts to become more important to creditors and lenders. They won't care as much about something that happened 5 years ago if you've been in great standing for the last 3 years and haven't had any mishaps.

Although the negative aspects of your report do expire after 7 years (sometimes 10, those pesky bankruptcies), keep in mind that the information can remain on file even past the expiration date. This information can be released under special circumstances, which is why it's important to get the negatives removed from your credit report if possible, rather than just wait it out.

So, overall, it's usually best left as a last resort when nothing else you've done has worked and no matter what you do you can't get the negatives removed from your credit report.

Disputing Accounts

Finding errors on your credit report and disputing them can have a huge impact on your credit score. Thus, you should make it a habit to check your credit report regularly for any errors so that you can deal with them. Remember that these mistakes may be costing you money, so it is in your best interest to get them resolved as quickly and as efficiently as possible. Let us now explore how you can do that in a detailed way and what the consequences and benefits of disputing accounts are.

If an account is incorrect on your credit report, it may exert a negative toll on your credit score, especially if the account includes negative information. Disputing these negative accounts will successfully raise your credit score almost immediately.

When it comes to account errors on your credit report, you should look for the following:

Negative information that is too old (older than seven years)

A derogatory mark on your credit report is supposed to be removed after a period of seven years has elapsed. If you have derogatory marks in your credit history which are older than seven years, you ought to dispute them and have them removed from your credit report.

Accounts which do not belong to you or incorrect account numbers

This is a big one. Obviously, the presence of any accounts on your credit report which you do not recognize, and which do not belong to you must be reported and disputed immediately. An account number that is wrong should also be disputed. If such errors on your credit report exist, then you may be a victim of identity theft, which can severely damage your credit score. If you suspect that this is the case, report this immediately to the credit bureaus and take other actions to protect your identity, such as freezing your credit cards, looking for any unusual or unauthorized charges, etc.

Another telltale sign of identity theft is if your credit report lists a residential address for you that you do not recognize.

Incorrect loan balances or credit limits

A credit limit that is incorrectly reported in your credit history ought to be corrected, because a wrong credit limit that is reported as being lower than it actually is will negatively affect your credit utilization ratio by lowering the overall amount of total credit that you have available in your name.

An inaccurate loan balance or credit balance that is too high will also negatively impact your credit score, since it raises the total amount you owe and thus increases your credit utilization ratio, which can have an impact on your credit score of up to 30 percent.

A credit card or a loan that still lists your former spouse

If you have a credit card or a loan that still has the name of your former spouse on it, you should try to have it removed. He or she may be racking up charges on that account that could be taking a negative toll on your credit score.

Incorrect account status (like a payment being wrongly reported as late)

If any of your accounts on your credit report have a wrong status, this could affect you negatively. For instance, if an account has reported to the credit bureaus that you have a late payment, this can negatively affect your credit score, because your payment history is a factor in the calculation of your credit score. So, an incorrectly reported payment history is something that you should watch out for on your credit report.

If you find that the account actually reported the late payment accurately, you can try to resolve the situation by contacting the creditor directly, offering to pay the delinquent amount, and asking if the delinquency can be removed or rescinded so that it will not show up any longer on your credit report and affect it negatively. And after you resolve the late payment in this fashion, make sure that the delinquency is removed from your credit report.

What Happens When You Dispute an Account?

The three credit bureaus each deal with a dispute in a slightly different manner. After you file a dispute, the three credit bureaus deal with the dispute in the following ways:

How TransUnion Deals with Disputes

TransUnion will inform you of the result of its investigation within thirty days of receiving your dispute. However, it can still take as long as forty-five days, so be prepared to wait until then. If the creditor or entity does not respond to TransUnion in the time allotted to it, then the credit bureau will delete the information that you disputed or correct it according to your request. As the investigation proceeds, a note, comment, or other such information regarding the dispute is not added to your TransUnion credit report.

How Experian Deals with Disputes

After you file a dispute of an account on your credit report with Experian, the credit bureau will contact the one who provided it with that information (usually the creditor). The creditor or entity who gave Experian the information that you are disputing has thirty to forty-five days from the time you filed your dispute to respond. After Experian receives a response, it will inform you of the result of its investigation. If the creditor or entity does not respond to Experian in the time allotted to it, then the credit bureau will delete the information that you disputed or correct it according to your request. As the investigation proceeds, a note, comment, or other such information regarding the dispute is not added to your Experian credit report.

How Equifax Deals with Disputes

After Equifax contacts and receives a response from the creditor or the entity, it will inform you of the result of its investigation. For Equifax, this happens on average within ten days of receiving your dispute. However, it can still take as long as thirty days, so be prepared to wait until then. If the creditor or entity does not respond to Equifax in the time allotted to it, then the credit bureau will delete the information that you disputed or correct it according to your request.

Unlike TransUnion and Experian, as the Equifax investigation proceeds, a note regarding the dispute is added to your Equifax credit report. It will have the following note on the disputed item: "Consumer Disputes—Reinvestigation in Process," a comment which your potential creditors will be able to see in your credit history if you apply for credit while the dispute is ongoing.

The Secret to Disputing Accounts with the Credit Bureaus

Here is the secret to disputing negative accounts with the three credit bureaus:

Be meticulous. Document everything with great care and make copies of everything. When you offer receipts and documentation as proof for your dispute, send copies, not the original documents. Also (we cannot emphasize this enough) file your dispute in writing, with an actual letter. Do not try to initiate a dispute online. Also, when you mail your letter, send it by certified mail and request a return receipt so you will receive a record of exactly when the credit bureau received your dispute. So, the secret to disputing accounts is to send everything in writing and be meticulous about documenting everything fully.

Send a Dispute Letter to the Credit Reporting Agency

The first thing you need to do is to send a dispute letter to the credit bureau. Here is how to do this:

Write a letter to the credit reporting company telling them that you wish to dispute inaccurate information or an inaccurate account on your credit report. You may choose to include a copy of your credit report that has the items which you are disputing circled or highlighted. After explaining exactly what on your credit report you believe is inaccurate, explain why you believe it is inaccurate and offer proof. The proof you offer should be copies of documentation that will lend support to your position.

Your letter to the credit bureau ought to have your full name (including your middle initial if you have one and any suffixes) and complete address. You should also include your social security number and the past addresses you have lived at within the last two years (or any that are associated with the items in question). Furthermore, your letter should include two forms of verification: one to verify your ID and the other to verify your address.

It should also clearly identify every piece of information in the credit report which you are disputing, list the relevant facts for each item and demonstrate why you are disputing that item, and make a request for the item to be corrected (in which case you must provide the correct information) or removed.

Send the letter using certified mail and pay for a return receipt. Also, make a copy of the dispute letter and of all that you enclosed within the letter. Do this for letter described in the following section as well.

Send a Dispute Letter to the Creditor or the Entity Who Furnished the Disputed Information

The next thing you need to do is to send a dispute letter to the creditor or the entity that provided the disputed information to the credit reporting agency. Here is how you can do that:

Write a letter to the entity who provided the incorrect information to the credit reporting company (usually your creditor) telling them that you wish to dispute inaccurate information or an inaccurate account on your credit report. You may choose to include a copy of your credit report that has the item which you are disputing circled or highlighted. After explaining exactly what on your credit report you believe is inaccurate, explain why you believe it is inaccurate and offer proof. The proof you offer should be copies of documentation that will lend support to your position.

Your letter to the creditor or entity who provided the disputed information ought to have your full name (including your middle initial if you have one and any suffixes) and complete address. You should also include your social security number and the past addresses you have lived at within the last two years (or any that are associated with the items in question). Furthermore, your letter should include two forms of verification: one to verify your ID and the other to verify your address.

It should also clearly identify the piece of information in the credit report which you are disputing, list the relevant facts for that item and demonstrate why you are disputing that item, and make a request for the item to be corrected (in which case you must provide the correct information) or removed. If the creditor or the entity who provided the disputed information finds that you are correct, it must report your dispute to the credit reporting company and ask it to remove or to correct the item in question.

The Bottom Line

That was a ton of information to digest, and indeed this topic alone could be (and is) the subject of a book in itself. But the key takeaways are the fact that because credit is an essential aspect of your overall financial health, you need to monitor your credit report and your credit score regularly so that you can get a full picture of how well (or poorly) you are doing financially. It has the added benefit of ensuring that you do not fall victim to identity theft. You should also check your report for any errors, which may be affecting your score in a negative way and correct them using the procedure described.

The FICO Score and VantageScore are two popular credit scoring models, and each of those takes slightly different things into consideration when calculating your credit score. Checking your credit score and credit report frequently will give you motivation to raise it (like a game or a challenge). And a higher credit score will lead to better, more advantageous offers (with lower interest rates and better terms) when you need a loan (for a car or a home, for example), a credit card, or a balance transfer. Thus, your overall financial health will be affected positively if you exercise vigilance when it comes to your credit score and your credit report. Also, because payment history and credit utilization ratio are two large factors in calculating your credit score, caring for your credit score will prevent you from paying any of your bills late and from running up too much debt on any one (or all) of your credit cards.

Chapter 4

DAY 2 – CONSIDER THE BENEFITS OF DEBT CONSOLIDATION AS A MEANS OF SIMPLIFYING THE PROCESS OF PAYING OFF YOUR DEBT

So, What Exactly Is Debt Consolidation, Anyway?

To consolidate your debt, in simple terms, is to combine multiple debts into a single payment. For instance, if you have five credit cards to pay off, debt consolidation would likely mean using a balance transfer offer to move all of the balances from the credit cards to one single credit card, on which you would make one payment per month. Or, it could mean taking out a loan and using the money from that loan to pay off the balance on all five cards completely; then you would make a payment each month on the loan.

Sometimes, debt consolidation can save you some money and make your life a bit easier. But that is not always the case.

What Are the Advantages and The Disadvantages of Debt Consolidation?

If you have a number of credit cards with high interest rates, it can save you money if you transfer all of those balances to a single, low interest card (or better yet, use a 0% APR balance transfer offer). Similarly, a loan may offer you a much lower interest rate than those credit cards, so it may save you money to use the money from the loan to pay off those high interest credit cards and pay only the loan instead. So, one advantage is that debt consolidation could save you money (if you do it carefully).

Another advantage is the fact that you are left with just one bill to pay (instead of having many to juggle). If you typically forget to pay one or more of your credit cards bills (or forget to pay even once or twice), you may benefit from having only one debt payment to make.

However, there are also several disadvantages. A balance transfer offer with a promotional 0% APR or a much lower APR than on your original cards is fine (and may be wise to take advantage of) *if you can pay the balance in full by the end date of the promotional offer*. If you do not carefully plan and budget to pay off the balance on time, the account will most likely charge you interest *from the date on which you first made the transfer.*

Also, a loan with a lower interest rate might sound good. But you must consider if you are saving money in the long run. If your loan has a lower interest rate but has a much longer term of repayment, you may end up paying quite a bit more than what you originally owed before you consolidated your debt. And you will be in debt for a longer period. So, if you choose to consolidate your debt with a loan, try to get a shorter repayment period (or make sure that there are no penalties for paying off your loan in advance). Sit down and take a little time to do the math to see how much you will save (if anything) by consolidating with a personal loan. Do not forget to consider any loan fees.

You should also beware of debt consolidation services or debt settlement services. They will often charge a host of hidden initial and monthly fees for doing something that you can easily do yourself. Just avoid them.

Should You Consider Consolidating Your Debt?

Consider debt consolidation to simplify the process of repaying your different kinds of debts. This way, you might benefit from better conditions, such as a significantly lower interest rate. But be sure to thoroughly consider both the advantages and the disadvantages of debt consolidation and determine if it will save you any money or cost you more

Does debt consolidation make sense for you?

If you have high interest credit cards and you are offered a promotional 0% APR balance transfer offer with a limit high enough to transfer all of your other balances with ease, then consolidating your debt in this way may make sense for you. But you must make sure that you will be able to afford to pay off the balance transfer offer before the promotional period ends. Look at the length of the promotion (oftentimes 9, 12, 15, or 18 months) and divide the total balance you are planning to transfer (including any balance transfer fees) by the number of months. That is the amount you will need to pay each month. See if you can realistically afford that. If you can, then this is a good way to save money on interest and fix a date for paying off your credit card debt.

But remember: if you fail to make a payment or if one of your payments is late, the penalties can be severe. You may even lose your 0% promotional rate and be charged the penalty APR as well as late fees. So DO NOT pay your bill late. Do whatever it takes to remind yourself to pay your bill on time (setting alarms every month, setting reminders, putting Post-It notes on the fridge, on your bathroom mirror, and on your computer screen, etc.). You can also set up auto pay, which will also lessen the stress regarding paying the proper amount on time. Just make sure you have enough in your bank account to cover the debit. And again, make sure that you are realistically able to pay off that balance transfer offer in full by the promotional deadline. If not, you will be charged a hefty amount of interest (starting from when you did the balance transfers).

Factors You Should Consider When Looking at Debt Consolidation

Do you tend to forget to pay at least one of your bills sometimes?

Is your paycheck not enough to cover all your bills?

Has controlling your spending failed to make a dent in the amount of debt you owe?

Are you ready (and disciplined enough) for a long-term commitment to rid yourself of debt?

If the answer to all four of the above questions is yes, then debt consolidation may in fact be the way to go for you. But remember to go into it with your eyes wide open and carefully understand the terms and conditions, as well as the length of your new debt obligation and how much money you will save in the long run.

Chapter 5

DAY 3 – FOCUS ON ONE KIND OF DEBT—THE SMALLEST DEBTS WITH THE HIGHEST INTEREST RATES

Focus on One Kind of Debt to Build Some Momentum and Give Yourself A Win

What kind of debt should you focus on?

If debt consolidation is not a viable approach for you, focus on one kind of debt (start with the smallest debts that are characterized by the highest interest rate). Although it seems counter-intuitive, it's about building momentum and giving your mind a win.

Make a list of all the debts that you owe

List out all your debts based on what is in your credit reports. It is important to get a full and clear picture of all the money that you owe and to whom you owe it. You may also wish to add up all your debts to get the sum of what you owe. Write that number down (along with the date) and commit to reducing that number over a set amount of time.

Seeing the list of all your debts will also help you to choose the debt that is one of the lowest amounts, but which has the highest interest rate.

Remember, you are going to focus on paying off one account at a time. Look at all the interest rates on all your accounts and circle the ones which have the highest interest rates. Among those, underline or highlight the one debt that has the lowest balance. This is the debt that you will focus on paying off first, your priority debt.

Be sure to keep making at least the minimum payment on all your other debts

Maintain minimal payments on other debts until you have that priority debt entirely covered.

If you fail to make a minimum payment on one of your other accounts, this will severely damage your credit history and lower your overall financial health, as you will incur late fees and a penalty APR. So, no matter what, you must make AT

LEAST the minimum monthly payment for all your bills ON TIME.

Your minimum monthly payments and other bills and necessary expenses (like utilities) are covered, the entire remainder of your income that month should go toward paying off that priority debt.

After paying off the first debt, move on to the next one

Once the priority debt is fully paid off, take that payment, and put it towards the next smallest debt with the highest interest rate. If you need to, go back to your list of debts, and reexamine all the debts that you circled. Cross out the debt that you paid off in permanent marker, and highlight the smallest debt remaining (of the circled debts).

Continue to build momentum by repeating this process

Keep building momentum and repeat the process. Every single priority debt that you pay off will feel great and be a psychological win for you. You will also be paying less interest each month (because you are paying off the high interest debts first) and will thus gradually have more and more money to go toward your debt payments, allowing you to pay it off faster than before. When, on your list of debts, you run out of circled items (having paid them all off and crossed them all off), circle the debts with the next highest interest rates. And so, on and so forth.

The Benefits of Paying Off Your Debt in This Manner

The Result

The result is you will finally be out of debt, after paying your debts off one by one. The large portion of your income that previously went toward paying your debts can now be used for saving and investing.

Why you should attack your debt using this method

Attempting to pay off several types of debt at the same time could lead to serious financial strain and could be disheartening. Attacking the debts that have the highest interest rates but also the smallest amounts will seem less daunting and paying off each one will give you a mental win and will constitute an achievable milestone. This is, of course, not the only way to pay off your debt. But we have found that it tends to be the most effective, since we human beings get encouraged when we see tangible progress and results. Being able to cross off your debts one by one in permanent marker is a very good feeling indeed.

Chapter 6

DAY 4 – KEEP WORKING ON REDUCING THE AMOUNT OF MONEY YOU SPEND EACH MONTH AND INCREASING THE AMOUNT YOU HAVE AVAILABLE TO PAY OFF YOUR DEBTS

Keep Reducing the Amount of Money You Spend Each Month to Increase the Amount of Money You Have Available for Paying Off Your Debts

Continue working on reducing your monthly spending, thus increasing the amount you can dedicate toward paying off your debts.

As you pay off each debt in the manner described in the preceding chapter, you will gradually have more and more money to dedicate toward paying off the next priority debt. But this chapter is all about cutting costs and saving money on your other expenses so that you can put *even more* money toward paying off debt. Obviously, the more money you save, the more money you will have available to pay off your debt, and the faster you will achieve your debt paying goals.

Ways in Which You Can Optimize Your Spending

Create a challenge for yourself

The simple fact of the matter is that people tend to enjoy winning. So, to motivate yourself to save money, you can develop a money saving challenge. Or several. It's up to you. For instance, you can challenge yourself to use enough coupons to save $10 every time you go to the grocery store. Or you can challenge yourself to save money on gas by driving around more efficiently. Figure out what works for you and give yourself a small reward or a pat on the back for successfully completing that challenge. Make a game out of it. It will make saving money that much easier and more fun.

Use an app

There are a few decent apps out there designed to help you save money. They work mainly because we like seeing results and tangible progress, and apps gamify saving money and make your progress more tangible.

Here are some of the best money saving apps:
- Mint
- Acorns
- Revolut
- YNAB
- My Budget Book
- Digit
- Tony Robbins Money
- PocketGuard
- SavingStar
- Prism
- Personal Capital
- Quicken
- Qapital
- Betterment

Cancel unnecessary subscriptions and be wary of online shopping

When we say cancel unnecessary subscriptions, we really mean to cancel them. Yes, that includes Netflix, Hulu, Disney+, Apple TV, and whatever other streaming services you household may subscribe to. And even your subscription to physical or digital newspapers or magazines. You will keep on living without them. We promise. You and your family may complain a bit, but once you get out of debt, if you budget for them properly, the return of such luxuries will be that much sweeter.

Also, be wary of online shopping. It is all too easy to spend money on Amazon and other online retailers, and they have tried their hardest to remove any and all barriers to buying. Sometimes, you can buy things with just a single click. Online shopping is a huge gateway to impulse buys, so try your best to cease this practice altogether. One practical way is to delete any credit card info you may have saved in your computer or on the retail website.

Do some research to save money on groceries

Groceries are, of course, a necessity, but there are numerous ways to save money on them. Do some research and take advantage of coupons, discounts, and loyalty or points programs. There is a great deal of savings, if you know where to look.

Optimize Your Spending (Head Over to Chapter Thirteen for More on This)

For more ways on how to save money and optimize your spending, head over to chapter thirteen.

Chapter 7

DAY 5 –TRY TO REDUCE YOUR INTEREST RATES AS MUCH AS POSSIBLE (WORK WITH YOUR CREDITORS TO DO SO IF YOU CAN)

Lower the Interest Rates as Much as Possible on The Debts You Owe

Work towards reducing interest rates if possible as you pay down your debt.

Why Should You Try to Lower the Interest Rates on Your Debts? What Are Some of The Benefits of Lowering Your Interest Rates?

Interest rates, as we discussed earlier, can be killer. Let's reiterate exactly how vicious interest rates can be in terms of getting you into and keeping you in debt, using another example:

Remember that the interest rate listed on your credit card statement or its terms and conditions is couched in annual terms as the APR or annual percentage rate. The daily rate (the APR on your credit card divided by 365) is multiplied by the balance on your account at the end of every day throughout the duration of the billing cycle.

For instance, if your credit card has an annual rate of 27.99%, the daily rate for your card would equal 0.07668%. If you have a balance of $10,000, you would be incurring interest of $7.67, resulting in a total of $10,007.67 on the following day. Recall that for most credit cards, compounded interest applies. This means that even if you spend no money on the following day, the interest for that day is charged on the $10,007.67, not the $10,000. You are paying interest on that interest. This continues as you keep carrying a balance on your credit card and purchasing more through the month's end. If you had a balance of $10,000 at the start of the month and did not make any other purchases or incur any other charges for the remainder of that month, you would end up having a credit card bill of $10,232.61 by the end of the month.

For the sake of illustration, if you incur no other charges on that credit card and make no payments on that card for the rest of the year, you will end up with a total credit card balance of $13.228.34 after 365 days. Now, the actual figure after one year would be less than that due to the fact that you would be making at least the minimum payment on the account each month; a credit card company would never let you get away with not making any payments on the account for an entire year. But do you see the dangers of interest and compounded interest? You do not just pay 27.99% interest on that $10,000 (which would equal $2,799). You pay more than 27.99% interest, since the interest is compounded. In the above illustration, you would pay $3,228.34 in interest after one year.

Let's see some more examples of how different interest rates can affect the total interest you pay. We will apply the same conditions as above, but with the following rates: 1) an APR of 23.99%, 2) an APR of 16.99%, and 3) an APR of 13.99%.

With an APR of 23.99%:

If your credit card has an annual rate of 23.99%, the daily rate for your card would equal 0.06573%. If you have a balance of $10,000, you would be incurring interest of $6.57, resulting in a total of $10,006.57 on the following day. Assuming the interest is compounded, if you had a balance of $10,000 at the start of the month and did not make any other purchases or incur any other charges for the remainder of that month, you would end up having a credit card bill of $10,199.09 by the end of the month.

For the sake of illustration, if you incur no other charges on that credit card and make no payments on that card for the rest of the year, you will end up with a total credit card balance of $12,710.50 after 365 days. In the above illustration (with its conditions applied), you would pay $2,710.50 in interest after one year.

With an APR of 16.99%:

If your credit card has an annual rate of 16.99%, the daily rate for your card would equal 0.04655%. If you have a balance of $10,000, you would be incurring interest of $4.65, resulting in a total of $10,004.65 on the following day. Assuming the interest is compounded, if you had a balance of $10,000 at the start of the month and did not make any other purchases or incur any other charges for the remainder of that month, you would end up having a credit card bill of $10,140.61 by the end of the month.

For the sake of illustration, if you incur no other charges on that credit card and make no payments on that card for the rest of the year, you will end up with a total credit card balance of $11,851.50 after 365 days. In the above illustration (with its conditions applied), you would pay $1,851.50 in interest after one year.

With an APR of 13.99%:

if your credit card has an annual rate of 13.99%, the daily rate for your card would equal 0.03833%. If you have a balance of $10,000, you would be incurring interest of $3.83, resulting in a total of $10,003.83 on the following day. Assuming the interest is compounded, if you had a balance of $10,000 at the start of the month and did not make any other purchases or incur any other charges for the remainder of that month, you would end up having a credit card bill of $10,115.63 by the end of the month.

For the sake of illustration, if you incur no other charges on that credit card and make no payments on that card for the rest of the year, you will end up with a total credit card balance of $11,501.30 after 365 days. In the above illustration (with its conditions applied), you would pay $1,501.30 in interest after one year.

As you can see, a different interest rate can have a vastly different effect on the total amount you owe. Securing a lower interest rate can save you hundreds or even thousands of dollars over time.

Thus, it is in your best interest to try to lower your interest rates as much as possible. An interest rate reduction of just a few percentage points can have a large effect in the long term.

Let's go over some of the methods for doing this:

Call Your Credit Card Issuers and Ask If They Would Be Willing to Reduce Your Interest Rate

This works (a lot of the time). Call your credit card issuers one by one and ask them if they can reduce your interest rate. That APR, unbelievably, is not set in stone. If you have a history of paying your bills on time, they may be willing to lower your interest rate as a gesture of good faith. You can even tell them that you are in the process of paying off your debts. Explain to them your plan for repayment. You can negotiate with them a bit. And if they refuse, you can always call again later. Explain how you deserve a lower interest rate because you now have a higher credit score (since you have been paying off your debt). You may find a friendly and sympathetic ear who is willing to lower your interest rate as much as the company will allow them to. Also, they may let you know of any 0% promotional balance transfer offers which are available to you if you give them a call and tell them your situation. This will go further toward helping you to save money and pay off your debt.

Consider A Balance Transfer Offer with A Lower Interest Rate (Or Even A Zero Percent Interest Rate)

You can also investigate a balance transfer credit card with a lower interest rate or even a 0% APR promotional interest rate. Remember the chapter on debt consolidation (Chapter 4)? Well, even if you decided that debt consolidation does not make sense for you, this does not mean that you cannot take advantage of a balance transfer offer. But instead of trying to consolidate all your debt using a balance transfer offer, you can just focus on transferring the balance from the credit card or cards which have the highest interest rates.

For instance, let's say you have 4 credit cards, each with a balance of $1,500. These four cards have the following APRs: 16.99%, 18.99%, 23.99%, and 27.99%. If you get a 0% promotional APR balance transfer offer in the mail, you should consider taking advantage of that. Transfer the balance with the highest interest rate first (27.99%). If you still have enough of the credit limit for your balance transfer card left over, transfer the balance for the card with 23.99% APR next. Just make sure that the balance transfer transaction fee is not too exorbitant. 2 to 4% is standard, but 5% is a bit steep. Make sure that the balance transfer will actually save you money (but if you are carrying a significant balance on a card with an APR of 20% or higher, transferring that balance to a 0% promotional APR card will almost certainly save you a lot of money, even when factoring in the transaction fee).

If you are following the method for paying down your debt described in Chapter 5, then once you have transferred the balance from the card with the highest interest rate to a 0% promotional APR card, you can focus on paying down the balance on the next highest interest rate card and make minimum payments on the balance transfer card. Just be sure not to miss any minimum payments and to have enough to pay off the entire sum before the promotional APR expires. A downside of taking advantage of a promotional balance transfer offer is that fact that oftentimes, if you have taken advantage of that offer on a credit card, any standard purchases made on that card will no longer have a grace period. This means that the card issuer will begin to charge interest on those standard purchases from the moment that you make them. Do not fall into this trap. If you use a balance transfer offer on a credit card, do not use that card for any other standard purchases, as they may accumulate interest immediately. You might even take the step of cutting up the physical card so that you do not charge anything to it accidentally.

Should you try to take advantage of a balance transfer offer or not?

Although there are some cons when it comes to using a balance transfer offer, you must thoroughly consider how transferring the credit card balances will affect your financial state. If such a move will save you money (after considering the balance transfer fee) and allow you to pay off your debt balance faster, then it is worth it to transfer the balance. But DO NOT miss any payments, and make sure that you can pay the balance in full by the end of the promotional period for the offer.

The Bottom Line Regarding Lowering Your Interest Rates and Taking Advantage of Balance Transfer Offers

Paying off debt requires a lot of self-discipline. If you aren't willing to go all the way through with paying off debt, don't do this step and just keep paying the smallest balance first, then the next, etc.

Chapter 8

DAY 6 – BE SURE TO PAY YOUR BILLS ON TIME

This step is crucial. We cannot emphasize enough just how vital it is that you pay your bills on time.

Make sure you are paying bills on time. This is one amazingly simple thing that can help you reduce the amount of debt you owe significantly. Setting up auto payments and other strategies that can help manage the overall budget. This is where building a budget (not just listing the debts owed) comes in. When you are paying off debt, you must make sacrifices and be more restrictive sometimes if you want to be debt free.

Be Sure to Pay Your Bills on Time – Even If You Are Able to Make Only the Minimum Payment

Recall that in Chapter 1, we advised you not to pay just the minimum amount due on a credit card. This is because paying only the minimum due will usually keep you in debt for a very long time, because you end up paying mainly the interest that is accumulating on your account rather than paying down a substantial amount of the principle.

So, we know that paying only the minimum payment on your credit cards is not a good idea. But you know what is even worse. *Failing* to pay even the minimum amount due on *even one* of your credit cards bills or loans. The minimum payment (on time and on every single one of your accounts!) is the *very least* you should pay. If you miss even a single minimum payment on any of your accounts, this can have drastically negative consequences on your financial health. Of course, you should try to pay more than the minimum amount due on your balances. But MAKE SURE that you pay AT LEAST the minimum amount due on each of your accounts ON TIME. We cannot emphasize this enough.

Why Should You Pay Your Bills on Time (No Matter What)?

Paying all your bills on time is a crucial factor when it comes to taking full control of your financial health and wellbeing. Knowing the exact dates of when all of your bills are due and making it a habit to pay each of those bills by the due date will go a long way toward saving you money, reducing your stress, boosting your credit score, and enabling you to receive offers for lower interest credit with more advantageous terms in the future.

Not only is paying your bills on time an excellent, essential practice that you should make a habit as soon as possible, but also the consequences of failing to pay your bills on time are exceptionally severe. Remember the credit score? Let's review how the FICO Score is calculated:

The five main factors used to calculate your FICO Score are payment history (35% of your FICO Score), credit utilization (30% of your FICO Score), length of credit history (15% of your FICO Score), new credit/number of accounts (10% of your FICO Score), and how your credit is mixed among types (10% of your FICO Score).

But what is the first, most important factor in calculating your FICO Score? Payment history! This counts for 35% of your score.

What does payment history mean again? Let's review:

Payment history is the history or the record of how you have made payments on the various lines of credit under your name throughout the time they have been in use. Payment history takes into consideration the various open credit accounts in your name, such as credit cards, personal loans, auto loans, retail credit accounts, mortgages, and more. This is the reason it is so crucial to be sure to keep track of all the accounts that are open under your name, so you can pay every account on time each month.

Payment history constitutes the biggest percentage (35%) of the five factors. So, if you miss even a single payment on an account, this can cause your score to drop considerably (by 100 points or more). And such a precipitous drop in your credit score (as well as a derogatory mark on your credit report) will detract significantly from your overall financial health and prevent you from getting credit offers with better terms.

Missing a payment or making a late payment will frequently trigger a late fee and a penalty APR, which is the exact opposite direction of where you want to go. Also, missing a payment on a balance transfer offer can cause you to lose the promotional rate! This is not something you want to happen to you if you are trying to pay down your debt.

Failure to pay that payment over a longer period can have even more severe consequences, such as sending the account into collections or your wages being garnished. These events will also serve to send your credit score into the dumpster.

We cannot emphasize this enough. Pay AT LEAST the minimum amount due on ALL your bills ON TIME (BY THE

DUE DATE). Just trust us on this one. Bad things will happen if you don't.

Methods to Make Sure That You Are Paying All of Your Bills on Time

Set calendar reminders and alarms for yourself for each of the bill payment deadlines

We live in the age of digital reminders. Take advantage of this. Sit down with your list of debts and set a reminder for every single payment due date. It doesn't matter whether you use a physical calendar, an iOS calendar, a Google calendar, or some other kind. Just do what works for you and make an event reminder for yourself for EVERY SINGLE bill due date. Set alarms for yourself to pay each one, if you need to do so. Better yet, contact all your creditors and have them move the due date to the same day (some date that's easy to remember, like the 1st of the month). Then, set as many alarms as you need to remind yourself to sit down with your list of debts before that day and go through the list, making each of the payments.

Many card issuers also have the option of email reminders, text reminders, and push notification reminders. Turn on whatever you need to keep yourself from forgetting to make all those payments.

Enroll in auto pay programs

Auto pay programs are an excellent way to keep you from ever forgetting to pay at least the minimum amount due for each of your accounts. If you are following the method of paying down debt described in chapter five, then set the auto pay amount for all of your other debts to the minimum due, and set the priority debt payment for an amount as high as you can afford.

The only problem with auto pay is that because you are no longer thinking too much about making payments, you may not be paying attention to whether your checking account has enough money to cover the payments. Returned check fees can be costly, and overdraft fees are costly as well. So, you should still set a reminder or alarm for yourself before your auto pay dates to remind yourself to check your bank balance to make sure that it is enough for paying all your bills.

Use a budgeting app or a budgeting software program

This is another great way to stay on top of your payments. Use a budgeting app. Sometimes this can be a savings app that also has a budgeting function. Here are some of the best ones (there is some overlap with the list of savings apps):

- Mint
- PocketGuard
- You Need a Budget
- Wally
- Mvelopes
- Goodbudget
- Simple
- Personal Capital

Figure out the total bare minimum you must pay each month

This one should be easy, since you already have your list of debts in front of you. Add up the minimum payments for all your accounts and figure out the total amount you need to pay (if you pay only the minimum due on each account). This will be the absolute floor for what you need to pay during the month. Of course, you will end up paying more than this, because you will be paying more than the minimum payment for your priority debt, but it is good to know the floor (beneath which you should never sink).

Lay Out the Terms of a Priority Based Spending Plan for Yourself—And Stick to It!

You need a budget. But don't think of it as a budget. Think of it as a priority-based spending plan. Right now (and until your debts are paid off) your priority is paying for your needs and paying off your debts, with little to no allowances for any wants.

Of course, the benefit of having a priority-based spending plan is that once you see where your money is going, you will be able to determine if you can afford to treat yourself to a small want once in a while.

Stick to your priority-based spending plan. This will require discipline. But it will be worth it in the end.

What Happens If You Do Not Pay Your Bills on Time? What Are the Consequences?

We cannot emphasize this enough. Pay all your bills on time (with at least the minimum due). Allow us to remind you of the severe consequences for not doing so:

Payment history counts for 35% of your FICO Score. So, if you miss even a single payment on an account, this can cause your score to drop considerably (by 100 points or more). And such a precipitous drop in your credit score (as well as a derogatory mark on your credit report) will detract significantly from your overall financial health and prevent you from getting credit offers with better terms.

Missing a payment or making a late payment will frequently trigger a late fee and a penalty APR, which is the exact opposite direction of where you want to go. Also, missing a payment on a balance transfer offer can cause you to lose the promotional rate! This is not something you want to happen to you if you are trying to pay down your debt.

Failure to pay that payment over a longer period can have even more severe consequences, such as the account being sent into collections or your wages being garnished. These events will also serve to send your credit score into the dumpster.

We cannot emphasize this enough. Pay AT LEAST the minimum amount due on ALL your bills ON TIME (BY THE DUE DATE). Just trust us on this one. Bad things will happen if you don't.

How to Undo Some of The Damage If You—Heaven Forbid! —Forget to Pay One of Your Bills on Time

If, for some horrible reason, you fail to pay a bill on time, do the following immediately:

Make a payment on the offending account as soon as you remember

Please. Just pay it as soon as you can (which should be the moment you realize that you missed the payment).

Call the creditor and beg them for forgiveness

You may think we are being a bit tongue in cheek here, but we mean it. After you have made a payment on that account, call the credit card company (the one whose payment you missed) and let them know that you made a payment for at least the minimum amount due already (and if you haven't done that yet, do that first—before you call the creditor). Be exceedingly apologetic and remorseful throughout the duration of the phone call. They will understand (but only once). You're only human. They might forgive you if you ask nicely (but only once). Ask them if they can waive the late fee which they may have automatically applied to your account. Also, ask them if they can ensure that your interest rate will remain the same (that is, that you will not lose your promotional interest rate or that it will not be increased to a penalty interest rate). And it doesn't hurt to ask to make sure that they continue to report your account to the credit bureaus as current (since you made a payment as soon as you remembered).

Chapter 9

DAY 7 – FIND A PARTNER WHO WILL KEEP YOU ACCOUNTABLE

Find A Partner Who Will Hold You Accountable

Find an accountability partner – your significant other, a friend or a coworker could help you maintain accountability and stick to your plan. Sometimes, it takes a little external push to achieve even your most ambitious goals.

Why Should You Find an Accountability Partner? What Should He or She Do for You?

Why you should find an accountability partner

Sometimes you may forget the fact that other people probably have the same feeling toward their debt as you do. So, when your buddies are going out for dinner for the fourth week in a row as you stay home in an attempt to save some money, it may seem to you that no one else has an understanding of what you are going through.

This is one reason having an accountability partner can be exceedingly helpful. Rather than feeling as though you are the only person who is struggling in this way, you have another person's shoulder on which to lean, someone else who will know exactly what you are going through.

Peer pressure can oftentimes be quite helpful, especially when it comes to paying off your debt

An accountability partner provides you with another slightly surprising motivation that you will be able to funnel toward getting rid of your debts more quickly: peer pressure. Although it bears a negative connotation, research has proved that peer pressure is an effective method to help a person achieve his or her goals. When your peers attempt a feat, you can use your desire to achieve what they achieve to motivate yourself toward the same goal.

So, if you tap into your instinctive need to fit in with others by using an accountability partner to reach your financial goals, then you will have a great deal more motivation for reaching said goals.

Here are a few things you ought to consider as you look for an accountability partner.

Choose your accountability partner with care

First, it is vital that you pick the right partner with whom to strive to pay off your debts. The tips that follow will not be effective unless you have paired yourself with the right accountability partner.

Your accountability partner needs to be a person whose opinion you have a regard for, someone who will not let you down and whom you will not want to let down.

Your accountability partner must be a person who will have your best interests at heart, one who will be able to be firm with you whenever it is necessary.

Find an accountability partner who fits the above criteria, or else none of the following strategies is going to be effective.

Lay down a series of ground rules

After you have found the right accountability partner for yourself, the two of you will have to lay down some ground rules when it comes to your credit card debt and your loans.

For instance, let us say that you desire to pay off your credit cards as fast as possible. In what time frame do you want to accomplish this? Do you have in mind a certain date?

As soon as each of you has a date in mind or a goal amount to pay off or to apply to your debt payments, then you will have to decide on the consequences which will be enforced upon you and which you will enforce on your accountability partner if you fail to meet your goals.

For instance, you might consider setting the following as a consequence: if one of you does not meet a certain goal, that one must then contribute to the loan or credit card repayments of the other person for that month.

No matter what sorts of consequences you choose, make sure that it is one which you will be highly motivated to avoid. But you should also ensure that it is not so extreme that you would not be able to handle it if it befell you.

Be sure to enforce your consequences

If the agreed upon consequences aren't enforced by you or your accountability partner, the partnership will fail. This is the reason you will need a person who is able to be tough on you when necessary. Choose someone who will be brutally honest when it comes to you and your debts.

This is where accountability can become difficult. Both you and your accountability partner need to be willing and able to follow through the consequences that you have laid out for one another. If either of you is not able to do so, then it is time to lay out some new consequences, or, potentially, a new accountability partnership.

Measure your progress together

As you and your accountability partner are both progressing toward paying off your debt faster, you should set up a few milestone goals along the way, so you are able to stay motivated as you go along. You should not have the final payment date as the only thing toward which you are working, or you run the risk of losing steam.

Thus, you should ensure that you are measuring your progress together with your accountability partner instead of simply reporting your progress to each other. This will keep both of you more committed to and focused on the journey and help you both to stay on top of things.

Celebrate when you meet milestones

It is true that an accountability partnership ought to have consequences, but that is not all it needs; it should have some celebrations as well. When you achieve the milestones that you have set for yourselves, you should find some ways to celebrate those achievements with one another, ways that will not cost you both a ton of money. You should revel in the victories and treasure the thought that another human being values your goals and your progress as highly as you.

This can serve to generate a deep bond between your accountability partner and you, a bond which will keep both of you motivated for your path ahead.

Additional Resources

- https://www.debt.com/how-to/stay-out-of-debt/
- https://www.debt.org/blog/10-mistakes-getting-out-of-debt/
- https://www.nerdwallet.com/blog/finance/10-ways-stay-debt/
-
  https://www.nomoredebts.org/blog/money/management/12-ways-to-get-out-of-debt
- https://moneyfit.org/blog/5-tips-stay-out-of-debt
- https://www.news24.com/fin24/Finweek/Personal-finance/how-to-get-out-and-stay-out-of-debt-20180511
- https://www.experian.com/blogs/ask-experian/credit-education/how-to-get-out-of-debt/

Chapter 10

A SUMMARY OF THE 7 DAY PLAN AND SEVERAL DEBT MANAGEMENT MISTAKES YOU NEED TO AVOID

That was quite a bit to digest, so in this chapter, we will give you a brief summary of the seven chapters we just went through, an overview of the full seven-day plan all in one place and a brief reminder of the significance of each day.

A Brief Summary of The Aforementioned 7 Day Plan

Day 1 – Check Your Credit Score and Credit Report in Order to Get A Sense of Where You Stand Financially

Check your credit score/report to get a better idea of your current situation. Also, it's important to make sure that your credit report is free from errors. This helps form a baseline of data to see how much debt you have and the whole picture before planning.

Day 2 – Consider the Benefits of Debt Consolidation as A Means of Simplifying the Process of Paying Off Your Debt

Consider debt consolidation to simplify the process of repaying your different debts. This way, you could benefit from better conditions, such as a more favorable interest rate or better or more manageable loan repayment terms.

Day 3 – Focus on One Kind of Debt—The Smallest Debts with The Highest Interest Rates

If debt consolidation is not a viable approach for you, focus on one kind of debt, (start with the smallest debts that characterized by the highest interest rate). Although it seems counter-intuitive, it's about building momentum and giving your mind a win.

Day 4 – Keep Working on Reducing the Amount of Money You Spend Each Month and Increasing the Amount You Have Available to Pay Off Your Debts

Continue working on reducing your monthly spending, increasing the amount you could dedicate to paying off debt.

Day 5 – Work with Your Creditors to Try to Reduce Your Interest Rates as Much as Possible

Work towards reducing interest rates if possible as they pay down debt. Communicate with your credit card issuer and inquire about an interest rate reduction. You can also investigate a balance transfer credit card with a lower interest rate or even a zero-interest rate.

Day 6 – Be Sure to Pay Your Bills on Time

This step is crucial. It cannot be emphasized enough just how vital it is that you pay your bills on time. Make sure you are paying bills on time; this is one very simple thing that can help you reduce the amount of debt you owe significantly. Setting up auto payments and other strategies that can help manage the overall budget. This is where building a budget (not just listing the debts owed) comes in.

Day 7 – Find A Partner Who Will Keep You Accountable

Find an accountability partner – your significant other, a friend or a coworker could help you maintain accountability and stick to your plan. Sometimes, it takes a little external push to achieve even your most ambitious goals.

Several Debt Management Mistakes That You Should Avoid at All Costs

Trying to borrow your way out of debt

Attempting to borrow your way out of debt simply perpetuates the vicious cycle of debt even more, due to the continuously compounding interest.

Failing to change your spending habits as you are trying to pay down your debt

Maintaining the same spending habits while trying to settle debt and ensure your financial stability in the future is a self-defeating proposition. If you keep up the same spending habits that got you into debt in the first place, then no matter how assiduously you stick to the rest of the tips in this book, you will fail to clear your debt. You may even end up in a worse place than you were before. So, if you are serious about paying off your debt, you will need to rein in your spending.

Selecting a debt relief (debt consolidation or debt settlement) program without fulling understanding the terms and conditions

Choosing a debt relief program because it sounds good, without understanding the terms and conditions, is another way to set yourself up for failure.

Failing to set up and maintain an emergency fund

A failure to set up an emergency fund (an essential that should happen while attempting to get out of debt, will be covered in more detail in one of the coming chapters) will also hamper your attempts to get rid of your debt.

Closing your credit card accounts as soon as they are paid off

This one may sound a bit counterintuitive. Closing your credit card accounts as soon as they are paid off may sound like a reasonable idea, but it is not so good for your financial health in the long run. Closing a credit card account will raise your credit utilization ratio, which will in turn have a negative effect on your credit score. So, if you know that once you pay off that credit card account, you will not be tempted to run up more debt on that card, you should simply leave it open. Fully paid off, but open.

Not keeping track of your progress

Failing to keep track of your progress when it comes to paying down your debt can be detrimental.

Waiting for a higher income before you start to pay off your debt

Waiting to start making more money before you begin repaying debt is also a big mistake. There is indeed such a thing as waiting too long.

Accumulating new debt just as soon as you get rid of the old debt

Planning to get out of debt just to start accumulating debt again once you are in the green will cause all your carefully planned debt settling efforts to be for naught.

Additional Resources

- https://www.thepennyhoarder.com/debt/accountability-partner/
- https://www.daveramsey.com/blog/6-people-you-need-while-getting-out-of-debt
- https://pennybros.com/get-accountability-partner-pay-off-debt/
- https://www.greatestworth.com/blog/thing-used-pay-off-debt-lose-20-pounds

Chapter 11

IF YOU DON'T KILL YOUR CREDIT CARD RIGHT NOW, YOU WILL HATE YOURSELF FOR IT LATER ON

Since far too many Americans are reliant on their credit card, it deserves a separate chapter. It's essential for readers to understand the perils of living on credit and the best ways to curb such unnecessary expenditure.

Your Credit Card Is One of The Biggest Culprits When It Comes to Enabling Your Irresponsible Spending Behavior

As mentioned in chapter one, you are probably spending more than you make. Your credit card is one of the biggest culprits contributing to such irresponsible behavior.

In 2020, The Average American Had $8,509 in Credit Card Debt!

Recall that the average credit card interest rate in the US as of June 2020 is 20.09% and the average credit card balance in the first quarter of 2020 was $8,509. The $8,655.39 the average American would owe after one month (which equates to $146.39 in interest), and the $10,401.69 the average American would owe after one year (which equates to $1,892.69 in interest for the year) is, as we discussed, a prime reason why so many Americans are in debt and stay in debt. Remember that those figures are based on a hypothetical situation in which no other purchases are made for the remainder of the year. And in Chapter 7 we extensively covered the effect that different interest rates can have on your account balance. Because the interest rates on credit cards is generally ridiculous (above 12% for most cards—with some cards going into the stratosphere with rates of 27.99% or even 30% or more!), it behooves you to get rid of your credit cards as quickly as possible by paying them off as quickly as you can.

Also, as you are paying off your credit card balance, consider leaving the physical card at home or getting rid of the physical card by cutting it up. Delete the card from your digital wallet so that you cannot spend with it. But remember, it is usually better not to close a credit card account after you have paid it off, due to the fact that closing the account will raise your credit utilization ratio, and a high credit utilization ratio will have a rather negative effect on your credit score.

What Are You Going to Do in Order to Stop Relying Excessively on Those Pesky Credit Cards of Yours?

So, what can you do to end your excessive reliance on a credit card?

Ask yourself why you use that credit card

Ask yourself why you're using a credit card. For most people, it's the lure of instant cash. This, however, isn't real money. It is a loan you will eventually have to pay back plus interest.

Leave your credit card at home

This is a simple one. Leave your credit card at home. Don't bring it with you. If it is not physically present in your wallet or your purse, you will have a lot harder of a time spending money on that card. But what about those digital wallets on your smartphone, full of credit cards that can be used wherever contactless pay is accepted? Delete them. If you are truly serious about paying off your debt and not accumulating newer and more crippling debt, remove your credit cards from your digital wallet and leave your physical credit cards at home. This will significantly hamper your ability to make impulse purchases.

In the very beginning and until you establish new healthy habits, being responsible with your spending is as simple as leaving your credit card at home. Just carry enough cash to last you through the day without enabling impulse purchases. Another approach you can rely on to curb spending in the beginning is pausing the credit card and deleting auto fill information from online shopping accounts (consider all ways to make the credit card inaccessible until you become more capable of resisting the temptation).

If you need some disposable income, get yourself a side gig

If you want to spend money on fun stuff, luxuries, and non-essentials, consider opportunities to boost your income (a second job, a side gig, a homebased business) so that you're only spending money that you have.

Consider canceling the credit card accounts that you don't need

If you have multiple credit cards, cancel the ones you don't need. However, be warned: cancelling all credit cards and closing the accounts is not a good idea as far as credit score building is concerned. But if you pay off one of your credit cards and you know that its mere existence is a temptation to you to run up more debt on it, then go ahead and cancel it.

Plan to switch to a debit card eventually

Make a gradual switch to a debit card – spending the money you've worked hard to earn is going to be harder.

Stop thinking of your credit card as your emergency fund

Your credit card is NOT your emergency fund! Instead, start thinking of other ways to build emergency cash. The all-important matter of an emergency fund is discussed in the following chapter.

Additional Resources

- https://www.frugalitymagazine.com/10-ways-stop-using-credit-card-80724/
- https://www.thebalance.com/how-to-stop-using-your-credit-cards-2385758
- https://www.thebalance.com/seven-tricks-to-stop-using-your-credit-cards-960384
- https://www.nomoredebts.org/blog/credit-cards/how-to-stop-relying-on-your-credit-cards-to-make-ends-meet
- https://www.moneymanagement.org/credit-counseling/resources/how-to-avoid-credit-card-dependence

Chapter 12

THE SECRET TO ENDING THE CYCLE OF DEBT

The fact of the matter is that sometimes, emergencies occur in life, and they can be exceedingly costly. Unexpected medical expenses, the loss of one's job, a major household appliance repair, divorce, a car repair—these and other such unforeseen expenses can contribute to massive financial strain. As we discussed earlier, even if you do not spend more money than you make, even one such emergency can cause you to fall into a potentially massive amount of debt—if you do not have an emergency fund that you can turn to in order to cover the expense. Having an emergency fund to offer a cushion against unexpected expenses can be lifesaving in such situations. And they can keep everyone from falling back into the cycle of debt.

The Secret to Ending the Cycle of Debt – The Emergency Fund

What Is an Emergency Fund?

So, what is an emergency fund? An emergency fund can be defined as a sum of money you have set aside to cover unexpected circumstances that do not fall within your regular monthly budget. Such circumstances could include a medical emergency, a sudden loss of your job or a reduction in your income, home repairs and replacements, car fixes, and the like.

As was stated earlier, an emergency fund generates a buffer for you financially which may help to keep you above water in your time of need without causing you to have to take out loans or to rely on credit cards. Such an emergency fund will allow you to stop borrowing more and getting yourself into more debt. However, few truly maintain an emergency fund.

Recall the following: Many Americans would not be able to pay their monthly expenses if they missed just one paycheck. And only 40% of Americans report that they could pay for an unexpected expense of $1,000, such as a car repair or a trip to the emergency room, using only their savings. Most people who were asked this question said that they would either take out a personal loan or put that expense on a credit card.

What's even more troublesome is the fact that most emergencies in the United States cost more than $1,000 to address. The average unforeseen expense was reported to be $3,500. Such situations are more common than we may realize. Last year, 28 percent of people had a financial emergency of some kind, and the tumultuous events of the first half of 2020 have served only to increase that number drastically. The US unemployment rate in April of 2020 rose to a record 14.7 percent, meaning that a record-breaking number of people that month experienced one of the costliest emergencies there is: losing a job.

Whether it is due to unemployment or some other reason, the fact of the matter is that due to the lack of a proper emergency fund, many Americans are just one personal emergency away from falling into debt. To get yourself out of this category, you must build up your emergency fund.

What Is A Good Size for Your Emergency Fund?

How big should your emergency fund be? A general rule of thumb is that your emergency fund should be sufficient to cover three to six months of basic expenses, which include essentials such as food, shelter, insurance, fuel, etc.). Even so, this is a generalization. The right amount is heavily dependent on your current income and your situation. Getting started with $500 to $1,000 is an excellent first step, and it's essential to keep on building the emergency fund (unemployment can be difficult to address and you'll need to have money to cover your monthly expenses for at least a few months).

A Step by Step Plan for Building Up Your Own Emergency Fund

Step 1 – Build up an emergency fund of $1,000 as you are paying down your debt

Build a $1,000 emergency fund while paying down your debt. That is essential to make sure you don't have to back track once the debt payoff momentum builds.

Step 2 – Figure out how much you can afford to set aside for your emergency fund each month

Determine a monthly sum you can dedicate to your emergency fund and do that first thing you receive your wage.

Step 3 – Start a coin jar

Start a coin jar at home – you'll be surprised to find out how quickly the cents will add up.

Step 4 – Use the services of a money saving app

Use an app that allows you to set some money aside every single month (Revolut has a vault but there are many other money management apps that have similar capabilities –

Step 5 – Deposit money automatically each month

Save through an automatic deposit.

Step 6 – Devote your tax refund to your emergency fund

Save your tax refund.

Step 7 – Reduce spending wherever possible

Cut spending where you can – even a few dollars per month can go a long way

Where You Should Keep Your Emergency Fund Money

In a bank account

This is a classic, safe choice that will give you a small interest rate on top of your deposits.

In a high yield savings account

This option is federally protected, and the money can be accessed quickly in the event of need.

In money market funds

This is another safe and highly liquid option.

Additional Resources

- https://www.nerdwallet.com/blog/banking/savings/life-build-emergency-fund/
- https://www.investopedia.com/personal-finance/how-to-build-emergency-fund/
- https://www.thebalance.com/easy-ways-to-build-emergency-fund-453608

- https://www.thebalance.com/easy-ways-to-build-emergency-fund-453608
- https://www.nytimes.com/2020/03/20/your-money/coronavirus-emergency-fund.html
- https://money.usnews.com/money/personal-finance/saving-and-budgeting/slideshows/how-to-build-an-emergency-fund

Chapter 13

SEE HOW EASILY YOU CAN SAVE MONEY AND BUILD SECURITY

Once debt has been handled, it's time to start setting longer-term goals. Saving money is possible in so many ways. The chapter will outline some effortless approaches to begin saving bit by bit (which will eventually lead to an avalanche-like effect).

First and Foremost, You Need to Set Goals That Are Realistic

The first and most important thing to do is set realistic goals. These should be based on your income and your spending habits. A goal you can achieve every single month will motivate you to start saving even more in the future.

Consider A Long-Term Goal in Addition to Your Short-Term Saving Goals

Once you have your short-term saving goals, consider a long-term goal, as well. Knowing how much you want to save in a couple of years and what you're going to use the money for can provide additional motivation to stick to healthy money management habits.

Increase the Amount of Money You Save By Identifying Spending Areas You Can Cut Back on Or Cut Out Completely

To gradually increase the money you are saving, you can also work on identifying spending areas you can reduce or cut out completely (eating out, entertainment, new clothes, new gadgets, etc.).

A Step by Step Guide to Saving Money for Beginners

Step 1 – Commit to saving at least a few dollars every month

Commit to saving a few dollars every single month, (even $5 per month in the beginning can make a difference). The goal here is to establish a habit you'll internalize and maintain.

Step 2 – Create a challenge for yourself

Create a personal challenge – the first month, find a way to spend $100 less. In a couple of months, you can increase the goal to $200 or even more. The money you save through this personal challenge should be allocated to your savings budget.

Step 3 – Use an app to help you save money

Use an app (Digit is one example) that will help you save money automatically.

Step 4 – Spend money wisely to save money

Spend money to save money (buying energy-efficient appliances for your home or a car that uses less fuel are two examples of expenditures that can produce an excellent return on investment through monthly bill reduction).

Step 5 – Think of ways that you can save on your utility bill

Find ways to bring down your utility bills even further – adjust the thermostat at home, conserve water, installing an on-demand tankless water heater (can deliver 30% savings in comparison to a standard water heater).

Step 6 – Figure out all the ways you can save money on groceries

Find ways to optimize your spending on groceries. Saving money on groceries and dedicating that sum to your savings account is fairly easy through a couple of changes – buy in bulk, opt for the store brand instead of a more expensive name brand, use coupons and cashback options, choose seasonal and local products, stick to a meal plan when doing grocery shopping.

Step 7 – Plan out any larger purchases well in advance (and factor them into your budget)

Always map out larger purchases in advance so that they don't break the routine you've just established.

Step 8 – Beware of online shopping and get rid of the subscriptions you don't need

Be careful with online shopping, and cancel unnecessary digital subscriptions – in 2019 alone, an average American spent $640 on digital subscriptions.

Step 9 – Always keep the bigger picture and your overall goal in mind

Since temptations surround you, make saving your priority by keeping a big goal in mind each time you feel pushed to buy something you don't really need.

Additional Resources

- https://bettermoneyhabits.bankofamerica.com/en/saving-budgeting/ways-to-save-money
- https://www.thebalance.com/the-complete-beginner-s-guide-to-saving-money-358065

- https://www.regions.com/Insights/Personal/Personal-Finances/budgeting-and-saving/10-Best-Ways-to-Save-Money
- https://www.lifehack.org/articles/money/anyone-can-saving-money-the-easy-way.html
- https://www.fool.com/how-to-invest/how-to-save-money-a-step-by-step-guide.aspx
- https://www.nerdwallet.com/article/finance/how-to-save-money
- https://creatingmyhappiness.com/6-steps-start-saving-money/
- https://www.businessinsider.com/personal-finance/how-to-budget-money-automate-savings-reach-money-goals-2020-5

Chapter 14

YOU DON'T HAVE TO BE A PROFESSIONAL INVESTOR TO BUILD WEALTH

So many people are afraid of investing because they believe financial operations are way too complicated to deal with. Luckily, investing small sums is possible and simple. The concluding chapter will give the reader some practical suggestions and tips that will ease their entry into the world of personal investments.

The Difference Between Saving and Investing

As someone who may be new to the world of investing, you may be unclear as to the fact that saving money and investing money mean completely different things. These concepts play distinct roles and have different purposes when it comes to your balance sheet as well as your financial strategies. Ensuring that you develop clarity regarding this fundamental distinction as you start your journey toward gaining financial independence and building wealth is crucial, because this will save you a great deal of stress and heartache. You are still liable to lose it all and fall into debt, even if you have a wonderful portfolio, if you fail to acknowledge how important it is to save.

There is a reason this chapter on investing comes *after* the chapters on keeping an emergency fund and on ways to save money. Once you have secured an emergency fund as was described in chapter four (or are well on your way to doing so) and have implemented the practices of saving money as outlined in chapter five, then and only then should you begin to invest. There is no point in investing if you have not already freed yourself of debt. There is also no point in putting money toward investments if you are liable to fall into debt at a moment's notice (that is, if you do not have an emergency fund to cover for unexpected expenses). The interest that will accumulate from unpaid debt far outweighs any gains you will make through investment, so it is vital that you pay off your debt and start saving money first before you think about investing. It's also a good idea to make sure that you have health insurance before you start investing, because a major (or even a minor) medical expense that is not covered by insurance will swiftly and easily get you into debt. The only exception to this rule is investing in a 401(k) plan in the case that your company will match those contributions.

What does it mean to save money?

Saving money is defined as the process of setting aside cash and placing it in very liquid (meaning it may be accessed or sold in a short amount of time—a few days at most) and safe accounts or securities. This may include savings accounts and checking accounts which are secured by the FDIC. This may include high yield savings accounts. This may also include United States Treasury bills. This may even include money market funds, if the structure of the fund allows for liquidity and safety.

Most importantly, your savings, your cash reserves, ought to be there as soon as you reach for them. They need to be available for you to grab, to take hold of, and to deploy immediately without much delay no matter what may be happening in your circumstances. Several famous investors even advocate having a stash of cash on hand in a place that you alone know of, even if it means taking a huge loss.

What does it mean to invest money?

Investing money is defined as the process of utilizing your money, or your capital, in order to purchase an asset which you believe has a decent probability of generating an acceptable and safe rate of return over time, which will cause you to become wealthier over time, even if it entails suffering some volatility, maybe even for a number of years. Also, true investments will be backed by a margin of safety of some sort, frequently in the shape of owner earnings or assets. Furthermore, the best types of investments are usually productive assets, like stocks, real estate, and bonds.

What Are Some of The Most Popular Investment Options?

Now that we have established that you should be saving money before you begin investing money, let us look at some of the most popular options for investing.

Individual Retirement Accounts (IRAs)

An Individual Retirement Account (IRA) is an investment tool that is tax advantaged which can be used by individuals to earmark, or designate, funds for retirement savings. As of the year 2020, there are different types of IRAs: traditional IRAs, Roth IRAs, SIMPLE IRAs, and SEP IRAs.

The advantages of a traditional IRA are the following:

Growth is tax-deferred

The contribution grows in a tax-deferred manner (until such time as you withdraw the cash) and you no longer need to pay taxes on that contribution while your money is increasing.

Contributions are deductible

Your contributions to a traditional IRA are deductible. This means that traditional IRAs are more useful if you believe you will be paying lower taxes when you are retired than when you are making your contribution.

Tax deductible

Your contribution to a traditional IRA is deductible yearly on your federal tax return for a period of 12 months.

Anyone with earnings can contribute

Anyone with earnings can contribute to a traditional IRA, but you are not allowed to contribute more than the amount of your annual earned income.

Inheritance allowed

You can pass an inheritance to your beneficiaries after your death.

More than one retirement account allowed

You can set up a traditional IRA even if you already possess another retirement plan. However, your contributions will not be completely tax deductible if you already have another certified retirement plan in place.

The disadvantages of a traditional IRA are as follows:

Low Contribution Limits

One of the major drawbacks to the IRA is the low maximum annual funding. If you are above 50, the maximum amount that you can contribute to a traditional IRA in 2019 falls between $6,000 and $7,000.

Taxable Distributions

With a traditional IRA, you will need to pay taxes when you take the cash out of your account. But this downside is frequently outweighed by the deduction you can take for your contributions in case you belong to a lower tax bracket when you retire than you did when you were making the contribution.

Also, you cannot just keep the money in your account forever to avoid paying taxes. Once you turn 70 and a half, you will be forced to make required minimum distributions (RMDs), which are withdrawals on an annual basis.

Early Withdrawal Penalties

Another huge disadvantage of a traditional IRA is the early withdrawal penalties, which occur if a distribution is taken before the age of 59.5; you will be forced to pay an added tax penalty of 10 percent unless you qualify for what is known as an early withdrawal exception.

Limitations based on Adjusted Gross Income (AGI)

The amount which is deductible is restricted according to your AGI and whether you participate in a retirement plan sponsored by your employer.

Your contribution may be fully deductible on your income taxes, partly deductible or not at all deductible in any way.

The other types of IRAs have slightly varying sets of advantages and disadvantages. Before you choose to place your hard-earned money in these types of accounts, be sure to educate yourself thoroughly.

Savings bonds

U.S. savings bonds are minimal risk investments. These savings bonds are offered by the U.S. Treasury directly, but they are not insured by the FDIC since they are backed by and owned directly by the full financial might of the U.S. government.

Mutual funds and ETFs

Mutual funds as well as exchange traded funds (ETFs) are popular types of investments found in retirement accounts, due to the level of diversification provided by them. Such funds offer a potential for higher returns on investment than Treasury bills, CDs, money market funds, and U.S. savings bonds. The drawback is that they carry a higher risk.

Mutual funds which are actively managed pool capital from investors and pay professional managers for investing in bonds, stocks, and other such investments. An index fund is a mutual fund which aims to duplicate the performance of a stock index, like the Standard & Poor's 500; they are managed passively.

Investments in stocks, funds, and bonds are not FDIC insured.

ETFs act similarly to index funds in that they will track an underlying index; however, unlike mutual funds, ETFs are traded like stocks. ETF shares are traded on a stock exchange, and investors can buy them and sell them for the duration of the trading day.

Stocks

A stock (which is also commonly known as equity) is a type of security which represents ownership in a fraction of a company or corporation. This gives the owner of that stock the right to a proportion of the assets and profits of the corporation that is equal to the amount of stock owned. A unit of stock is called a share.

Stocks are predominantly bought and sold on stock exchanges, although there may be private sales of as well; stocks are frequently the foundation of the portfolios of most individual investors. Such transactions need to conform to regulations set by the government and designed to safeguard investors from any fraudulent practices. Historically, stocks have outperformed many other types of investments in the long term, although they can be considered a riskier form of investment. Stock can be bought from online stockbrokers.

Bonds

Bonds are defined as a debt obligation which will mature on a particular date. Bonds also pay the bearer interest through coupon payments at a stipulated rate. Agencies like Standard & Poor's and Moody's provide you with ratings on certain bonds. Bonds can be traded around the world, and it is possible for you to lose money through them.

Certificates of deposits (CDs)

Certificates of deposit (CDs) are a very safe type of investment, which, like savings accounts, are insured by the FDIC. Funds invested in CDs are typically locked in for a period which can range from three months to several years. CDs usually pay interest at a higher rate than savings accounts.

Real estate

Investment real estate is defined as real estate which does not function as a primary residence, but which serves to generate income or is intended for the purposes of investment. Some investors prefer investing in real estate because they are investing in something physical and tangible, as opposed to something intangible like securities. Real estate investment yields come from capital gains (because of the likely increase in value of the property over time) and or from rental income. Real estate is a way for investors to diversify their portfolios. However, the disadvantages of real estate investments include the fact that they require a significant amount of money upfront, the fact that they are not at all liquid (cannot be converted to cash quickly or easily), and the fact that one may have to spend much of one's time dealing with tenants and managing and/or repairing the property.

Precious metals

Precious metals are something else in which individuals can invest their money. They include gold, platinum, silver, and other valuable commodity materials. Individuals can invest in precious metals by holding actual bullion in the form of coins or bars, by trading in the futures market, through mining companies, through mutual funds, and through ETFs.

Cryptocurrencies

A cryptocurrency is defined as a virtual or digital currency which is secured through cryptography, making it almost impossible to double spend or counterfeit. Most cryptocurrencies are comprised of decentralized networks which are based on blockchain technology, which is a distributed ledger that a disparate network of computers enforces. A prominent feature of these cryptocurrencies is this: they are usually not issued by a central authority of any kind, which renders them theoretically immune to manipulation or interference by the government.

Investors who would like to trade cryptocurrencies will require a place to store them in the form of a digital wallet. Buying the cryptocurrency is achieved by connecting your digital wallet to a credit card, a debit card, or a bank account. Investors in cryptocurrencies can become part of an online marketplace or an exchange to trade such cryptocurrencies.

Taking Your First (Successful) Steps into The World of Investing

Start small

There are micro investing platforms that you can test out with a couple of bucks each month before moving on to a more serious opportunity.

Plan thoroughly

Plan, plan, plan – choose a sum of money that you feel comfortable investing, and which is not going to impact your monthly budget.

Figure out the timeframe for your investment

You should also determine the timeframe of the investment. Will you be saving for retirement? Will you need the money 10 years from now? 20? That timeframe will determine which investment options make the most sense in terms of meeting your goals.

Consider a 401(k) plan

One of the simplest options for getting started with investing is the 401(k) plan. Speak with your employer about this option, as your company may match your contributions to your 401(k) plan.

Understand the risks that come with investing

Understand that all kinds of investment come with a risk. High risk investments bring high returns but the losses can also be significant. This is why you need to build a diversified investment portfolio that will cancel out some of the risks. If you have no idea how to get started with that task, talking to an investment consultant would be wise.

Figure out strategies for reducing the fees that come with investing

Consider the fees associated with common types of investment and assess strategies for reducing those.

Don't fall for things that sound too good to be true

Stick to true, tested, and effective investment methods. If something appears too good to be true, it probably is. Exaggerated promises and exceptional "returns" are often linked to an investment scam.

Educate yourself thoroughly on all the risks before wading in

Educate yourself before jumping into something risky – learning more about investments is not that challenging, especially if you rely on the right educational materials.

Investing will get easier over time

In time, you will find it a lot easier to continue investing and diversifying your portfolio. The money already in your investment account will be earning some interest, and the bigger the sum gets, the higher the returns will be. These returns can further be invested in an additional opportunity to give you peace of mind and even more stability.

Resist the temptation to cash out too early

Don't be tempted to cash out your investment too early – there are short term risks that could lead to a reduction in profitability, but such drops are typically offset over time.

Additional Resources

- https://money.usnews.com/money/personal-finance/family-finance/slideshows/a-beginners-guide-to-investing-9-easy-steps-to-get-you-started
- https://www.listenmoneymatters.com/investing-for-beginners/
- https://www.nerdwallet.com/article/investing/how-to-start-investing
- https://investorjunkie.com/getting-started-investing/
- https://corporatefinanceinstitute.com/resources/knowledge/trading-investing/investing-beginners-guide/
- https://medium.com/datadriveninvestor/investing-for-beginners-a-simple-guide-to-get-you-started-5a7281fafd65

CONCLUSION

What You Learned from Reading This Book

So, what have you learned from reading this book? You learned the basics regarding why people get into debt, including the number one reason (which nobody likes to admit), that people spend more money than they make.

You also learned a basic need for paying off debt: to have a change in your mindset regarding the concept of debt as well as your spending habits.

You then were equipped with a comprehensive, step by step and day by day approach for getting out of debt. This step by step plan was broken into seven days, one chapter per day.

Then, you discovered the debt management mistakes you should avoid so you don't jeopardize your path to building wealth and financial stability.

You also learned about the danger of credit cards, as well as how to wean yourself from these financial traps.

Next, you found the secret for *staying* out of debt: an emergency fund. You also gleaned some excellent tips on how to save money.

Finally, you received some practical and altogether doable tips on wading into the world of investing, which will help you to achieve your long-term goal of building wealth and financial security. Careful planning and sticking to reliable, tried and true investment strategies will be the key to your investment success.

Some Key Takeaways

Spend less than you make.

You need a change in your mindset.

Check your credit score and credit report.

Pay off debt by attacking the lowest amount of debt with the highest interest rate first.

Pay all your bills on time (with at least the minimum due).

Save wherever possible; care for needs, not wants.

Reduce your interest rates as much as you can by contacting your creditors and taking advantage of balance transfer offers (carefully).

Find an accountability partner.

Build up an emergency fund!

Once you are out of debt, build wealth carefully by investing prudently and with thorough planning and budgeting.

Now That You Have Read This Book, What Should You Do Now?

Now that you have all the necessary tools for your financial success and well-being, go out there and put them to good use! Remember that a key ingredient for financial success is using the tools in this book. You have a plan of action. Now is the time to execute it. In other words, do it. If you don't do it, the words in this book will be of no avail.

If you enjoyed the book and feel that it has been or will be helpful to your future financial health, please leave a review on Amazon.

Simple¢ents

What Did You Think?

First, thank you for purchasing this book. More importantly, thank you for reading it all the way through!

At SimpleCents, we know you literally have millions of choices on what books you want to read. We are so extremely grateful you decided to pick this one up. Our dedicated team of writers and personal finance educators hopes it added value to your life. If you got just one small nugget that could push your finances forward, we'd loved to hear from you and ask that you take 60 seconds to post a review on Amazon. Your review will have a direct impact on how we continue to craft our books for future readers. And, we actually read them too…seriously.

We know you might not think it's a big deal to not leave a review, but no joke, it's a big deal. Your potential review is so important to us being able to continue to get our education out to people like you who want help. Amazon sees your review and gives us a boost so it can be seen by those people.

We wish you the best in your personal financial future!

P.S-Don't forget to check out your FREE BONUSES on the next pages! You won't want to miss out on it!

FREE BONUS VIDEO COURSE!

The Set It And Forget It Money System

How 4 Easy Steps In Less Than 33 Minutes Will Set Your Money On Autopilot Without Spending Hours On A Budget Even If You Hate Tracking Your Finances

http://www.SimpleCentsMoney.com/VideoCourse

SimpleCents

The Secret of Getting Your Finances on Track

If you've read all the way through this book, you're probably serious about changing the results in your personal finances

One "secret" of success that most people forgot about is the power of association. Having a community of likeminded people to support, encourage and challenge you is like putting nitrous oxide in your car's engine....you're gonna get to where you want to go a whole lot faster with it.

We want to give you that opportunity by giving you the opportunity to join the private SimpleCents Facebook group!

This is an exclusive group only available for SimpleCents readers.

Share your struggles, your victories, what's helped you and what you need help with. Everyone has a story, so come share yours and inspire others on the journey with you!

https://www.facebook.com/groups/simplecentscommunity

About SimpleCents

SimpleCents is passionate about helping the average person master their money. Their mission is to provide practical personal finance advice for everyday situations. Whether it's rebuilding your credit score, getting out of debt, or taking the fear out of investing your money, SimpleCents is built on timeless principles to help you succeed.

SimpleCents is all about sticking to the basics: keep your dollars and cents simple. That's why you won't see any individual authors names on your books. They purposely stay anonymous, so you know that it's about helping you, not their individual reputations.

SimpleCents is based Texas and was officially formed in 2019.

REFERENCES

A. (2020, February 27). 10 examples of poor financial money management | Personal Finance Blog. Retrieved from https://moneyjourneytoday.com/poor-financial-money-management/

Action, C. (2019, January 2). Consumer Action - Minimum Payment Warning. Retrieved from https://www.consumer-action.org/helpdesk/articles/minimum_payment_warning

Briseno, T. (2020, January 27). What's the No. 1 reason people go into debt? Retrieved from https://money.howstuffworks.com/personal-finance/debt-management/reason-people-go-into-debt1.htm

Burnette, M. (2020, March 20). Emergency Fund: What It Is and Why It Matters. Retrieved from https://www.nerdwallet.com/blog/banking/savings/life-build-emergency-fund/

Chen, J. (2020, July 2). Investment Real Estate. Retrieved from https://www.investopedia.com/terms/i/investmentrealestate.asp

Comoreanu, A. (2020, June 24). Credit Card Debt Study. Retrieved from https://wallethub.com/edu/cc/credit-card-debt-study/24400/

Compound Daily. (n.d.). Calculator. Retrieved from https://compounddaily.org/calculator/

Dixon, A. (2019, November 19). A growing percentage of Americans have no emergency savings whatsoever. Retrieved from https://www.bankrate.com/banking/savings/financial-security-june-2019/

Equifax. (n.d.). Why Should I Check my Credit Reports and Credit Scores? Retrieved from https://www.equifax.com/personal/education/credit/score/why-check-your-credit-reports-and-credit-score/

Fortney, L. (2020, March 16). How to Invest in Bitcoin. Retrieved from https://www.investopedia.com/articles/investing/082914/basics-buying-and-investing-bitcoin.asp

Frankenfield, J. (2020, May 5). Cryptocurrency. Retrieved from https://www.investopedia.com/terms/c/cryptocurrency.asp

Insler, S. (2017, March 3). How to Use the Buddy System to Pay Off Student Loans Faster. Retrieved from https://studentloanhero.com/featured/accountabilit y-partner-pay-student-loans/

Investopedia. (2019, December 19). What Are Examples of the Most Common Types of Investments in an IRA? Retrieved from https://www.investopedia.com/ask/answers/102714 /what-are-some-examples-most-common-types-investments-ira.asp

Investopedia. (2020, May 27). Understanding Credit Card Interest. Retrieved from https://www.investopedia.com/articles/01/061301.a sp

Kennon, J. (2020, March 27). The Difference Between Investing and Saving and Why You Should Do Both. Retrieved from https://www.thebalance.com/saving-money-vs-investing-money-358062

Leonhardt, M. (2020, January 22). 41% of Americans would be able to cover a $1,000 emergency with savings. Retrieved from https://www.cnbc.com/2020/01/21/41-percent-of-americans-would-be-able-to-cover-1000-dollar-emergency-with-savings.html

Money Management International. (n.d.-a). Debt Consolidation. Retrieved from https://www.moneymanagement.org/debt-consolidation

Money Management International. (n.d.-b). Ultimate Guide to Consolidating Your Debt | MMI. Retrieved from https://www.moneymanagement.org/budget-guides/consolidate-your-debt

Nova, A. (2019, January 23). A $1,000 emergency would push many Americans into debt. Retrieved from https://www.cnbc.com/2019/01/23/most-americans-dont-have-the-savings-to-cover-a-1000-emergency.html

The Smart Investor. (2020, July 7). Traditional IRA Pros and Cons. Retrieved from https://infoforinvestors.com/money/retirement/traditional-ira-pros-cons/

White, A. (2020, April 20). What happens when you miss a credit card payment? Retrieved from https://www.cnbc.com/select/what-happens-when-you-miss-a-credit-card-payment/

Made in the USA
Columbia, SC
15 March 2022

57727127R00093